W9-ABE-512

THE JAPANESE THROUGH AMERICAN EYES

THE JAPANESE THROUGH AMERICAN EYES

Sheila K. Johnson

Stanford University Press
Stanford, California • 1988

Stanford University Press
Stanford, California

© 1988 by Sheila K. Johnson
Portions of this book were originally published,
in somewhat different form, in *American Attitudes
Toward Japan, 1941–1975* (Washington, D.C.: American
Enterprise Institute, 1976), © 1976 by Sheila K.
Johnson, and in *Amerika-jin no Nihon-kan* (Tokyo: Simul
Press, 1986), © 1986 by Sheila K. Johnson

Printed in the United States of America

CIP data appear at the end of the book

Preface

WHEN I FIRST spent a year in Japan, in the early
1960s, I vowed I would never write about it. To begin with,
Japan was my husband's chosen field of study, and as a young
wife I was determined to demonstrate my independence of mind.
But I had also read all the standard English-language academic
works then available on Japanese culture and society—books by
Sir George Sansom, Ruth Benedict, and Edwin O. Reischauer,
for example—as well as many of the popular books about
flower arranging, the tea ceremony, kabuki, and sumo. And even
though I had been trained as a social anthropologist, it seemed
to me that much of what I was reading promoted a dangerously
antiquarian and exceptionalist image of the Japanese. Sometimes they were depicted as cruel warriors driven by a spartan
code of ethics called *bushido*. At other times they were seen as
harmony-loving worker bees, or perhaps as otherworldly aes-
thetes. Many books labored hard to explain how the Japanese
could actually be all three: the argument was that they were a
very contradictory, not to say schizophrenic, people.

Partly in reaction to this viewpoint, I decided that the Japanese were probably not so different from people everywhere.
Such an approach also has an honorable history in anthropol-

ogy, where some scholars concentrate on strange customs while others are more drawn to the study of cultural universals. At the time, my "flat-footed" approach to Japanese culture led to some insights that have since become "common knowledge." While many of my colleagues were still bemoaning the low status and powerlessness of Japanese women, I became convinced that Japanese women actually had a great deal of power and independence in the management of their homes and families. And where there were superficial differences between Japanese and American ways of doing things, the end result often seemed much the same. For example, in America women usually learn to drive a car at an early age because this is their ticket to freedom: henceforth they are no longer dependent on fathers, boyfriends, or husbands to take them places (nor do they need to reveal where they are going). In Japan, I discovered, a woman often learns to drive to be of service to her family. But once she has dropped off her husband at the train station and her child at school, she is as free to "do her own thing" as her American counterpart.

I also heard a great deal, in those early years, about the superiority of the Japanese family system in caring for the elderly. I later went on to write a book about working-class retired people in the United States and discovered that the American family was not nearly as fragmented as many scholars then thought. Many of the elderly people I interviewed lived within a ten to thirty minutes' drive of at least one of their adult children. Among professional people, older parents and their children may live farther apart—the parents in Florida or Arizona and the children in New York or San Francisco. But here, too, strong ties are maintained via telephone and airplane. The current extended family system in America often looks chaotic and *ad hoc,* but it persists and is guided by universal ties of duty and affection.

Over the years, I have observed similar developments in Japan. Traditional values which dictated that the oldest son should live with and care for his parents are being replaced by a more flexible system, in which care for elderly parents is shared by several children or devolves upon the most financially able child or the child with the closest emotional ties to the parents. Instead of the strained relationship that often exists between a wife and her husband's mother, one now sees many more examples of a widowed mother's spending her last years in her daughter's house. Moreover, given Japan's increased urbanization and the tendency of many married couples to live in small apartments, it seemed inevitable to me even twenty-five years ago that fewer elderly people there would be able to live with their children at all. Instead, I predicted that solutions similar to those in the United States would be found: elderly parents living in a small apartment next door or in the same neighborhood as their children, or in special apartment complexes designed so they can live independently but still receive medical care and supervision when necessary. In other words, I saw the "graying" of Japan as developing along lines very similar to patterns in other advanced industrial societies.

I mention some of these ideas because they grew out of my conviction that the Japanese are an interesting but not necessarily *sui generis* people. Nonetheless, I continued to resist writing about Japan, since I was not a trained Japan specialist and to write a "popular" work about the country would be to join the very stream of literature that I found so misleading. In 1973, however, I wrote an article about American attitudes toward China.[1] As a result, I was invited to do a similar piece about American attitudes toward Japan. This struck me as an interesting idea, and the study that resulted was published by the American Enterprise Institute in 1975.[2]

My research into the world of popular American attitudes toward Japan often surprised and shocked me. I had decided to study such attitudes as they were expressed in best-selling novels and non-fiction, and I was not prepared for the harshness of the books and articles written during and immediately after World War II. (Since I grew up in German-occupied Holland, the wartime imagery I had imbibed dealt almost exclusively with the Nazis. In fact, I did not really know there was a war with Japan until the autumn of 1945, when my mother's sister returned, gaunt and withdrawn, from a prisoner-of-war camp in the Dutch East Indies.) Nor did I find it easy to account for the powerful grip the Pacific War still had on the American imagination. It may be that this fascination will lessen as the generation that fought the Japanese dies out, but it is equally possible that this war, like the Civil War, will continue to haunt Americans more persistently than either Korea or Vietnam.

It was the recurrence of best-selling books about the war with Japan that made me realize my study could not take a simple chronological approach. I had thought that American attitudes toward Japan from 1941 to the present would fall into several well-defined periods. Instead, I found that certain mutually contradictory themes seemed to recur, and that these themes, in defiance of logic, were often simultaneously present in American thinking or even in the mind of a single person. Years later, I was dismayed but no longer startled when the *New York Times,* on the fortieth anniversary of the war's end, published a vicious article by Theodore White comparing Japanese business practices of the 1980s to Japanese behavior during World War II.

When my earlier study of American attitudes toward Japan was first published in 1975, it attracted some favorable comment; but Japanese-American relations did not then seem to many people a particularly salient issue. Attitudes on both sides of the Pacific were generally positive; tourism and trade were growing but in a balanced way. My final substantive chapter dealt with the "business nexus," but in 1975 there were no best-sellers about business, and instead I relied on impressions gained from magazine and newspaper articles to gauge American attitudes.

Ten years later the picture had changed quite considerably. Whereas American novels and nonfiction of the 1950s and 1960s brought us geishas and cherry blossoms, the novels of the late 1970s and early 1980s brought us shoguns and ninjas.

Suddenly, large numbers of books were being published in the United States that analyzed Japanese business practices and recommended them to American companies. One of these—William Ouchi's *Theory Z*—even became a best-seller.

By 1987, there were also growing numbers of books and articles that were highly critical, even fearful of Japan. If one recalls that Ruth Benedict called her famous study of Japan *The Chrysanthemum and the Sword*, then it is fair to say that in the early postwar period Americans concentrated on the chrysanthemum, seeing Japan as an artistic, somewhat feminized nation; in the late 1970s and 1980s, however, Americans began to focus more on the sword, recalling Japan's more masculine, assertive, samurai tradition.

Such a shift in popular imagery may not be a wholly bad thing. Immediately after the war, Americans and Japanese alike naturally wanted to bury the bad memories of a conflict that had cost them both a great deal. But such repressed memories must sooner or later be brought into the open, and in doing so Japanese and Americans may come to view each other with greater honesty and equality. On the other hand, if the second image—of cold-blooded, inflexible samurai—comes to dominate American thinking about Japan, then the two nations may once again find themselves in a situation reminiscent of the 1930s, when each country blamed the other for its policies in a self-reinforcing cycle of recrimination.

But there are grounds for optimism. American attitudes toward Japan have changed enormously over the past half century. I believe this would not have been possible if such attitudes were, in fact, based on something as long-lasting and deeply rooted as national character. If American attitudes toward Japan were an accurate reflection of the Japanese essence, then one would have to believe that from 1941 to 1945 the Japanese were devils, that they were then rapidly transformed into angels, and that today they may be en route to becoming devils again. I do not think this is possible; therefore, I assume that popular stereotypes are greatly influenced by immediate events. If this is so, then nations have the ability to affect and change how they are perceived by others.

I do not know how or when the current friction between the United States and Japan over trade issues will be resolved. But I do know that once it is solved in a mutually satisfactory way, American attitudes toward Japan will improve overnight. There is a huge reservoir of positive imagery about Japan on which Americans can draw. There is also much interest among Japanese about how they are perceived by Americans. When much of this book was translated into Japanese in 1986, it made a brief appearance on *their* best-seller list, an amusing development for someone who had undertaken to gauge popular opinion by scrutinizing best-sellers.

This book owes a great deal to the encouragement of Donald C. Hellmann of the University of Washington, Seattle, who commissioned the original study, and to Frank Gibney of the Pacific Basin Institute in Santa Barbara, who urged me to bring it up to date. I am also grateful to several anonymous readers who spotted errors and lacunae in the manuscript. But my greatest intellectual debt is to my husband, Chalmers Johnson. He first awakened my interest in Japan by taking me there, and his own work in the field has been a major source of knowledge and inspiration for me. Needless to say, however, no one but the author is responsible for the statements and opinions in this book.

S.K.J.

Contents

THE JAPANESE THROUGH AMERICAN EYES

ONE

The Ambiguous Legacy

AMERICANS, IT SEEMS, have always been ambivalent about Japan. Commodore Perry's men found the Japanese to be "the most polite people on earth"; yet Perry was deeply frustrated by what he considered to be their outright lies, evasions, and hypocrisy. As Foster Rhea Dulles has commented, this bifurcate impression—of courtesy and hypocrisy—"helped to set a pattern of American thinking about the Japanese that has persisted for a century."[1] Lafcadio Hearn, one of the great romantic boosters of all that was Japanese, nevertheless lamented in a private letter:

But with what hideous rapidity Japan is modernizing, after all!—not in costume, or architecture, or habit, but in heart and manner. The emotional nature of the race is changing. Will it ever become beautiful again? Or failing to become attractive, can it ever become sufficiently complex to make a harmony with the emotional character of the West?[2]

Hearn also knew the cost of the old character and society, whose passing he lamented: "The old kindliness and grace of manners need not cease to charm us because we know that such manners were cultivated, for a thousand years, under the edge of the sword. . . . And this immemorial doctrine of filial piety—exacting all that is noble, not less than all that is terrible, in duty, in gratitude, in self-denial."³ In still a different mood, he reflected on the comment of another foreigner, a friend, who had said to him, "If those people [the Japanese] could only feel for us the sympathy we feel toward them!" "Indeed," noted Hearn, "the whole question of life in Japan to a sensitive westerner was summed up in that half-utterance. The unspeakable absence of sympathy, as a result, perhaps, of all absence of comprehension, is a veritable torture."⁴

These early comments and thoughts reveal a great jumble of ambivalent feelings that has certainly not lessened during the last half century of American contact with Japan. The war, followed by the occupation, followed by a period of expanding tourism and trade, followed by a period of serious trade imbalances marked by mutual recriminations between the two countries— all these have left their imprint on American attitudes. In 1973, when several college classes were asked to free-associate about Japan—to complete the sentence "When I think of Japan, I think of . . ."—the words that tumbled out included: small, fierce country; transistors; Hiroshima; geisha girls; beautiful trees and topography; Tokyo and traffic jams; kimonos; high degree of industrialization. And they tumbled out in no particular combinations: that is, a person who mentioned the tea ceremony might also mention transistor radios and cars, and someone who thought of ink-brush painting might also think of kamikaze. When asked to name three prominent Japanese, past or present, the students most frequently mentioned Tojo, Emperor Hirohito, and Prime Minister Tanaka; but some students thought of Bashō, Toshiro Mifune, and Kenzo Tange.

The sociologist Nathan Glazer has suggested that responses of this sort reveal two things: first, that American attitudes toward Japan are, in fact, quite shallow—that most Americans do not think much about Japan at all, and that their impressions are therefore likely to be hasty and contradictory; and second, that their ambivalence is an accurate reflection of the paradoxical nature of Japan and the Japanese—that, in the words of Ruth Benedict,

The Japanese are, to the highest degree, both aggressive and unaggressive, both militaristic and aesthetic, both insolent and polite, rigid and adaptable, submissive and resentful of being pushed around, loyal and treacherous, brave and timid, conservative and hospitable to new ways. They are terribly concerned about what other people will think of their behavior, and they are also overcome by guilt when other people know nothing of their misstep. Their soldiers are disciplined to the hilt but are also insubordinate.[5]

I do not happen to think that either of Glazer's contentions about the origins of American attitudes is precisely accurate. American perceptions of Japan strike me as no more shallow than American perceptions of France, Spain, or Russia. In fact, they may be more profound, since they tend to be based on wartime experiences, tourism, or contact with Japanese products, from kimonos to automobiles. (What words would the average American associate with Spain, for example, and what prominent Spaniards might he be able to name other than Franco or Picasso?) Neither do I think that Japanese character is so inherently contradictory that it necessarily elicits an ambivalent response. Japanese character differs markedly in certain respects from American character, and this difference may simultaneously attract and repel Americans. But this is not at all the same thing as saying that the Japanese character harbors such a galaxy of traits that one can only respond with confusion.

Another possible explanation for American ambivalence toward Japan is a simple situational one. Most middle-aged Americans have experienced during their lifetimes a whole range of attitudes toward Japan called forth in succession by changing historical situations: rage and fear during World War II, pity and compassion during the occupation, admiration and curiosity during the late 1950s and 1960s, followed by a return to fear (this time of Japan's impact on American industries) mixed with appreciation for her products during the 1970s and 1980s. None of these feelings, moreover, entirely superseded the preceding ones; instead they overlie one another in the complex pattern we see today. Nor does any one individual or social group in America display the entire range of feelings toward

Japan. An individual's feelings will be influenced by age, sex, political persuasion, education, and the nature of his or her contact with Japan. This diversity of opinion also tends to register on questionnaires and surveys as ambivalence.

Nevertheless, the question of whether there is a relationship between Japanese national character and American perceptions of Japan and the Japanese is an important one that cannot be lightly dismissed. All studies of prejudice and national stereotyping must at some point deal with the "kernel of truth" hypothesis—the notion that underneath all the psychological and social reasons why one group of people may call another ethnic group lazy, dirty, musical, greedy, or sly, there is a basis in fact. During World War II, Americans perceived Japanese as sneaky, cruel, and fanatical; had anyone had the temerity to ask them *why* they felt this way, they would have answered "Because the Japanese *are* sneaky, cruel, and fanatical." Today, many Americans think of the Japanese as intelligent, hard-working, and competitive, and these same Americans would no doubt be prepared to defend their opinions by citing evidence that the Japanese are, in fact, all these things. Those who are disturbed by the disparity between our wartime and present-day opinions are merely told that the Japanese have changed—that losing the war and being forced to become democratic during the occupation did them a world of good. Unfortunately, there is no evidence that the Japanese temperament has changed radically. The considered opinion of most psychologists, anthropologists, and sociologists is that prewar and postwar Japanese share certain recognizable characteristics—call it "national character," if you will—and that wartime studies merely emphasized the dark side of these characteristics, whereas postwar studies have focused on their more positive aspects.

Wartime National Character Studies

It is an unfortunate fact that the entire field of national character studies—or "studies of cultures at a distance," as they were sometimes called—began as an adjunct of World War II. To be sure, the intellectual roots of such studies lie in the 1920s and 1930s, when Freudianism had a profound impact on American anthropology and when a number of anthropologists began administering psychological tests in primitive societies and applying psychoanalytic interpretations to some of their cultural data. With the start of World War II, however, many of these same scholars went to work for the Office of War Information or other branches of government, where they began applying their techniques not merely to complex societies but to societies with which the United States was then at war. The practical purposes of these studies were to discover what might break the morale of the German or Japanese soldier, what sort of propaganda might work best among the occupied nations of Europe and Southeast Asia, and what sort of occupation policies the United States should implement once it had won the war.

In the case of Japan, most of the anthropologists and psychologists who set out to delineate its social and character structure had never been to Japan, could neither read nor speak Japanese, and had no deep prior acquaintance with the history or culture. This list would include Geoffrey Gorer, Gregory Bateson, Margaret Mead, Ruth Benedict, Weston LaBarre, Alexander Leighton, and Morris Opler. Two exceptions were Douglas Haring, an anthropologist who had lived in Japan from 1917 to 1922 and again from 1924 to 1926, and John Embree, an anthropologist who had married an American woman born and raised in Japan and who, from mid-1935 to late-1936, lived in a small Kyushu village about which he wrote a village study that is still considered a classic.[6]

It would be wrong to imply that the differences that developed between these scholars—and the differences that a present-day reader sees in their work—can be explained entirely in terms of the intuitive, "deeper" knowledge of the old Japan-hand versus the more schematic, perhaps superficial knowledge of the armchair scholar. One of the more sensitive and still highly regarded works to come out of these wartime efforts was Ruth Benedict's *The Chrysanthemum and the Sword*, which was based entirely on her reading of novels and secondary sources, her viewing of Japanese movies, and her interviews with *issei* and *nisei* (first- and second-generation Japanese-Americans). But Ruth Benedict was a special sort of scholar—a woman who was also a poet, who came to academic life late, and who in all her work revealed a gentle and perceptive judgment. But not all of those who were studying Japan from a distance, in the midst of a bitter war, were similarly endowed. Thus the basic analysis of Japanese character came to rest on the notion that harsh toilet training and an emphasis on shame rather than guilt had pro-duced a nation of individuals who were obsessively clean, polite, and obsequious, but that "behind the rituals of the individual obsessive can always be discovered a deeply hidden, unconscious and extremely strong desire to be aggressive," and that "the sanctions for correct behavior in a Japanese environment would be no longer operative in a different environment and under dif-ferent circumstances; and consequently all the aggression and cruelty which is unsuitable in Japanese contexts can be allowed vent." [7]

In a postwar article, John Embree protested that a number of the childhood training practices on which such national charac-ter analyses were based were practices he had never observed during the course of his fieldwork in Japan. He went on to ar-gue that

In much of the character structure writing about the Japanese there is an ethnocentrism which fitted in well with the social needs of the war period during which the "scientific" conclusions as to their character were made. Racist interpretations were socially as well as scientifically unacceptable at this time but "character structure" interpretations were all right and served just as well in the literate world to "explain" the international and domestic behavior of Japan.[8]

Douglas Haring, also writing after the war, suggested that much of the behavior that Gorer and others called "compulsive" and blamed on harsh toilet training could be better explained in terms of Japanese history. Haring argued that the Japanese had lived, since the beginning of the Tokugawa period (1603), under a form of government that stressed strict sumptuary laws and correct social behavior, enforced by an efficient network of political spies and samurai. (This is a point also made by Lafcadio Hearn.) In the period extending from 1868 to 1945, the samurai were replaced with a centralized police force, but the average Japanese reacted in the same, learned way.

All the features of the alleged "compulsive personality" of the Japanese are logical fruits of the police state. An explanation centered in diapers is suspect if it neglects three centuries of fear-inspired discipline. To say this does not refute psychoanalytic interpretations, for relentless police supervision modifies the human psyche profoundly. . . . Police controls impose strains on individuals—strains that multiply and become more rigorous as adulthood is reached.[9]

The great virtue of the Embree-Haring approach is that it frees us of some of the wartime biases of national character studies without throwing out the baby with the bathwater—that is, without denying that our perceptions of the Japanese may have some basis in reality. As Embree has pointed out: "A summary (even when accurate) of a nation's citizens' behavior traits, while of some value in predicting individual behavior of members of the society, does not provide a magic explanation for a nation's aggressive warfare, whether it be Japanese, British, American, or Russian."[10] We should therefore be able to look at some of our reactions to the Japanese during the war, and later on, without constant reference to what may or may not be their basic personality. If we do that, it will become clear, I think, that many of our reactions are situational—they are responses to immediate acts and circumstances—and that where we are reacting to the Japanese qua Japanese we are, often as not, reacting merely in terms of how they differ from ourselves. For example, the Japanese are generally speaking more reserved than Americans, a national character trait that may strike us as either politeness or aloofness, depending on how favorably disposed we happen to be at the time; but the fact that we react to this quality of reserve is probably conditioned by our own less formal style of behavior.

The Migrating Asian Stereotype

There is one other ingredient that enters into the perceptions Americans have of the Japanese, and this is their concurrent perceptions of the Chinese. Since both nations are Asian and therefore somewhat strange to Americans, superficial similarities have sometimes led to a sort of ideological lumping together of the two. This generalized Asian stereotype can also extend to Koreans and Vietnamese. During the Korean War and again during the Vietnam War, all the old World War II epithets applied to the Japanese resurfaced: gooks, slopeheads, slant-eyes, yellow devils, and so on.

One study of wartime American attitudes toward Japanese-Americans argues that in part the Japanese-Americans simply inherited the prejudices that had built up against Chinese immigrants during an earlier period:

One popular method [of transferring this prejudice] was to attribute to the Japanese all the alleged crimes of the Chinese by emphasizing their similarities—and then to point out their differences as compounding the felony. Thus the United States Industrial Commission reported in 1901 that the Japanese "are more servile than the Chinese, but less obedient and far less desirable. They have most of the vices of the Chinese, with none of the virtues. They underbid the Chinese in everything, and are as a class tricky, unreliable and dishonest." [11]

A more disturbing tendency in recent times has been the development of two polar-opposite stereotypes about Asians, which

Chinese   *Japanese*

HOW TO TELL YOUR FRIENDS FROM THE JAPS

Of these four faces of young men (*above*) and middle-aged men (*below*) the two on the left are Chinese, the two on the right Japanese. There is no infallible way of telling them apart, because the same racial strains are mixed in both. Even an anthropologist, with calipers and plenty of time to measure heads, noses, shoulders, hips, is sometimes stumped. A few rules of thumb—not always reliable:

▶ Some Chinese are tall (average: 5 ft. 5 in.). Virtually all Japanese are short (average: 5 ft. 2½ in.).

▶ Japanese are likely to be stockier and broader-hipped than short Chinese.

▶ Japanese—except for wrestlers—are seldom fat; they often dry up and grow lean as they age. The Chinese often put on weight, particularly if they are prosperous (in China, with its frequent famines, being fat is esteemed as a sign of being a solid citizen).

▶ Chinese, not as hairy as Japanese, seldom grow an impressive mustache.

▶ Most Chinese avoid horn-rimmed spectacles.

▶ Although both have the typical epicanthic fold of the upper eyelid (which makes them look almond-eyed), Japanese eyes are usually set closer together.

▶ Those who know them best often rely on facial expression to tell them apart: the Chinese expression is likely to be more placid, kindly, open; the Japanese more positive, dogmatic, arrogant.

In Washington, last week, Correspondent Joseph Chiang made things much easier by pinning on his lapel a large badge reading "Chinese Reporter—NOT *Japanese*—Please."

▶ Some aristocratic Japanese have thin, aquiline noses, narrow faces and, except for their eyes, look like Caucasians.

▶ Japanese are hesitant, nervous in conversation, laugh loudly at the wrong time.

▶ Japanese walk stiffly erect, hard-heeled. Chinese, more relaxed, have an easy gait, sometimes shuffle.

Carl Mydans, Black Star

Chinese   *Japanese*

can be pasted like labels onto either the Japanese or the Chinese (or the Koreans or Vietnamese), as the occasion warrants. The favorable Asian stereotype includes such attributes as patience, cleanliness, courtesy, and a capacity for hard work; the unfavorable one emphasizes clannishness, silent contempt, sneakiness, and cruelty. There is a good deal of evidence that these two stereotypes alternate between the Japanese and the Chinese, and that when one nation is being viewed in the light of the favorable stereotype, the other will be saddled with the unfavorable epithets. An example of the blanket Asian stereotype, combined with the denigration of the Japanese as opposed to the Chinese, can be found in the December 22, 1941, issue of *Time* magazine in which readers are told "How to tell your friends from the Japs."

Scholars working on national character studies during World War II were not immune to such polarized views. The psychologically oriented anthropologist Weston LaBarre wrote two important papers setting forth "Some Observations on Character Structure in the Orient"—one dealing with the Chinese, among whom he had spent some two years as a liaison officer attached to General Stilwell's headquarters, and the other dealing with the Japanese. He began his paper on the Chinese by confessing, "It is nearly impossible for an American who has first-hand acquaintance with the Chinese not to develop for them and for their civilization an affection and a profound respect"; he then proceeded to assert that "despite all provocations and all their many wars, the Chinese have never become militaristic," and "the Chinese are not imperialistic . . . [they] have never had the evangelical impulse to carry their values to other peoples and to impose these upon others by conquest." Moreover, "Americans and Chinese are alike in their fundamental extroversion," and "American and Chinese civilizations are natural and inevitable allies." Not surprisingly, LaBarre found the Japanese to be compulsive, self-righteous, fanatical, arrogant, and suspicious.[12]

It goes without saying that a few years later one can find examples in which these stereotypes are completely reversed. The Chinese have become fanatical, cruel, and militaristic, whereas the Japanese have demonstrated themselves to be compliant, gentle, and peace-loving. Shortly after the Chinese entered the Korean War, General MacArthur, who only a few years before had praised the Chinese for their devotion to the cause of free-dom, was telling Elizabeth Gray Vining, "I can't throw these educated, carefully nurtured [American] boys against hordes of coolies."[13] The notion that pro-Chinese attitudes correlate with anti-Japanese attitudes, and vice versa, has even been explicitly formulated on occasion: when Charles Poore reviewed John Hersey's *Hiroshima*, he tried to protect Hersey from still anti-Japanese Americans who might regard the book as too sympa-thetic to Japan: "John Hersey would be among the last to favor the Japanese. He happens to have been born in China, which gives him a natural dislike for the Japanese that goes back to his childhood days."[14]

In 1973, when China was still in the throes of the Cultural Revolution, the chief images that the word China evoked among a class of college students were "Mao, communist repression, mass conformity, ignorance, small people all wearing the same blue outfits and screaming slogans." At the same time Japan was seen in much more favorable terms: "money, cars, and transistor radios; industrious, hard-working people; beautiful country-side." Twelve years later, the images of China had become much more positive. Although the overwhelming impression was of China's huge size and population, her people were described as "hard-working, family-oriented, dedicated, and tranquil." When asked to name three prominent Chinese, 85 percent still re-sponded with Mao, but other names mentioned were Deng Xiao-ping, Chiang Kai-shek, Chou En-lai, Sun Yat-sen, Confu-cius, and Bruce Lee.

Japan, in 1985, was described almost exclusively in terms of modernization and industrialization: high-tech, electronics, au-tomobiles, robots. Wartime images (kamikazes, Hiroshima) and traditional culture images (pine trees, geisha, tea ceremony) had both declined; but when asked to name three prominent Japanese, the most frequent name was Emperor Hirohito (30 percent) or a wartime figure (Tojo, Yamamoto, Hirota). Thirty-five percent of the respondents could name *no* Japanese at all. Many still perceived the Japanese as industrious, intelligent, and polite, but some saw these traits as aggressiveness, chauvinism, and cunning.

The seesaw correlation of American attitudes toward Japan and China—when one is up the other is down—strikes me as further evidence that perhaps we are reacting to something Asian, something different from ourselves, and that the particular coloration we attach to a given country is dictated by current political considerations or events of the recent past. For this reason, I propose to put aside the ultimate question of what the Japanese are or are not, and to look instead at what Americans have thought and felt about them over the past forty-five years and what sorts of occurrences seem to have shaped those thoughts and feelings.

Approaches to the Study of Attitudes

The study of attitudes can be approached in a variety of ways, one of the most obvious being via the public opinion poll. I myself conducted two such polls among classes of college students enrolled in Political Science 2 at the University of California, Berkeley. Although the course dealt with comparative politics, it did not focus on Asia, so one may assume that the students were not self-selected to have an interest in either China or Japan. Nonetheless, my respondents were clearly not representative of the U.S. population as a whole in either age or background. (For one thing, 17 percent of the 1973 group and 22 percent of the 1985 group were of Asian ancestry.)

Between July 16 and 21, 1985, the *New York Times* and CBS News sponsored a much more extensive and scientific poll on

American attitudes toward Japan. In it 1,569 adults in every state except Alaska and Hawaii were interviewed by telephone.[15] This poll revealed some interesting views, and I shall be referring to it from time to time. But the problem of how to interpret popular attitudes on the basis of responses to specific questions, and the greater problem of how to square such attitudes with actual behavior, remain. For example, 63 percent of those questioned favored either quotas on Japanese products, an import surcharge, or an out-and-out boycott of Japanese goods. But only 12 percent favored imposing such sanctions if it led to retaliation by Japan, higher prices, and diminished product choices. Meanwhile 60 percent of those surveyed said they had recently bought a Japanese product, 30 percent believed that Japan made more technologically advanced consumer products than the United States did, and sixteen percent said they owned a Japanese automobile.[16] Obviously, the gap between consumer behavior and publicly stated attitudes toward Japan is quite large, and consumer understanding of how economic sanctions against Japan would actually affect the American economy is not well developed.

Another approach to the study of attitudes is via the pronouncements of "opinion leaders." This is the approach taken by Nathan Glazer, who analyzed the writings of Ruth Benedict, Edwin Reischauer, Zbigniew Brzezinski, and Herman Kahn, in an effort to discover what sorts of informed impressions have shaped American thinking.[17] Unquestionably, the views of opinion leaders have an impact on a small elite—including, from time to time, government policymakers. To the extent that the opinion leaders have their ideas translated into policy—an example would be the wartime anthropologists' conclusion that the Japanese emperor should not be forced to abdicate or be tried as a war criminal—or widely disseminated via the popular media, they may also shape public opinion. But the route is very indirect, and it is by no means readily apparent which ideas and controversies shaking the academic world are going to gain wider currency. Benedict's *The Chrysanthemum and the Sword*, considered a classic in its field, sold only 28,000 hardback copies (a high-priced paper edition was not published until 1967) between 1946 and 1971. This amounts to a sale of about 1,000 copies a year, most of them no doubt going to professional anthropologists or college students taking courses on Japan. However, one gains some sense of the impact of this book when one reads in Ian Fleming's *You Only Live Twice*:

[Tiger Tanaka] has acquired an *on* with regard to me. That's an obligation—almost as important in the Japanese way of life as "face." When you have an *on*, you're not very happy until you've discharged it *hon*orably, if you'll pardon the bad pun. And if a man makes you a present of a salmon, you mustn't repay him with a shrimp. It's got to be with an equally large salmon—larger, if possible—so that then you've jumped the man, and now he has an *on* with regard to you, and you're quids in morally, socially, and spiritually—and the last one's the most important.[18]

It was passages such as this, distantly based on Ruth Benedict's analysis of *on* and *giri*, that led me to a third approach to the study of popular attitudes: a survey not of what the elite reads but of what is read by the general public—popular magazines, newspapers, and those few books that "break out" of the confines of a narrow audience-appeal to become best sellers. In order to see what such an approach might yield, I began by compiling a list of all the books dealing with Japan that have appeared on the *New York Times* best-seller list for more than one week since 1941 (see Table 1). The lists are based on sales figures in bookstores across the country, and a compilation drawn from them reveals a good deal about popular American interest in and knowledge of Japan. For one thing, it reveals how pervasive and lasting has been the American preoccupation with the war in the Pacific. Best-sellers about the Japanese and World War II began with John Hersey's *Men on Bataan* in 1942 and Richard Tregaskis's *Guadalcanal Diary* in 1943. But books about the war continued to be best-sellers well into the 1980s.

It was the evidence of continued interest in the Pacific War

TABLE I

Best-sellers Dealing with Japan, 1942–1987

Year	Author/title	Weeks on list
1942	John Hersey, *Men on Bataan*	26[a]
1943	Richard Tregaskis, *Guadalcanal Diary*	26[a]
1944	Joseph Clark Grew, *Ten Years in Japan*	22
1946	John Hersey, *Hiroshima*	5
1948–49	Norman Mailer, *The Naked and the Dead*	62
1951	John Gunther, *The Riddle of MacArthur*	18
1952	Elizabeth Gray Vining, *Windows for the Crown Prince*	27
1954	James Michener, *Sayonara*	21
1954	Robert Theobald, *The Final Secret of Pearl Harbor*	8
1954	Charles Willoughby and John Chamberlain, *MacArthur, 1941–1951*	7
1955	Michihiko Hachiya, *Hiroshima Diary*	9
1956	Courtney Whitney, *MacArthur: His Rendezvous with History*	6
1957	John Marquand, *Stopover Tokyo*	13
1957	Walter Lord, *Day of Infamy*	17
1957	Gwen Terasaki, *Bridge to the Sun*	4
1958	Alice Ekert-Rotholz, *The Time of the Dragons*	16
1958–59	"Pappy" Boyington, *Baa Baa Black Sheep*	37
1960	Elizabeth Gray Vining, *Return to Japan*	4
1961	Oliver Statler, *Japanese Inn*	23
1962	John Toland, *But Not in Shame*	4
1964–65	Ian Fleming, *You Only Live Twice*	23
1964–65	Douglas MacArthur, *Reminiscences*	30
1967–68	Walter Lord, *Incredible Victory*	21
1975–76	James Clavell, *Shōgun*	32
1978–79	William Manchester, *American Caesar*	33
1980	Eric Van Lustbader, *The Ninja*	22
1980–81	William Manchester, *Goodbye Darkness*	20
1981	William Ouchi, *Theory Z*	22
1982	Gordon Prange, *At Dawn We Slept*	19
1982	John Toland, *Infamy*	7
1983	Gordon Prange, *Miracle at Midway*	4
1984	Eric Van Lustbader, *The Miko*	9
1984–85	Studs Terkel, *"The Good War"*	22
1986–87	David Halberstam, *The Reckoning*	26

SOURCE: *New York Times* best-seller lists, 1941–87. For a somewhat different compilation, which includes best-sellers about China and southeast Asia, see Daniel B. Ramsdell, "Asia Askew: U.S. Best-Sellers on Asia, 1931–1980," *Bulletin of Concerned Asian Scholars*, 15 (Oct.–Dec. 1983), 2–25.

[a] Approximate (figures not published weekly).

that first led me to suspect there might be certain themes in American attitudes toward Japan, themes that ebb and flow but that are never entirely absent from any given period. My original intention had been to treat American attitudes toward Japan chronologically—the war, the occupation, the late fifties, the "Reischauer years" (1961–66, when Edwin Reischauer was American ambassador to Japan), and so forth. To a certain extent, of course, the themes that I have drawn from popular literature do emerge chronologically: the "Madame Butterfly theme" (see Chapter 5) arises during the occupation, although its origins can be traced back to the original story of Madame Butterfly as well as to Lafcadio Hearn; and the great American infatuation with traditional Japanese culture that began with the tourist boom of the late 1950s and early 1960s also has antecedents in Lafcadio Hearn and Ernest Fenollosa. But themes, regardless of when they emerge, have a tendency to persist. The theme of Hiroshima, for example, runs through the late 1940s, '50s, and '60s like a recurring refrain.

In pursuing the themes that I believe have shaped American thinking about Japan during the past half century, I have not stuck exclusively to the best-seller list. I have also looked at a great variety of articles in popular magazines. Many of the best-selling books also appeared in magazines, to reach an even wider audience. For example, John Hersey's *Hiroshima* first appeared in *The New Yorker*, and Elizabeth Gray Vining's *Windows for the Crown Prince*, Gwen Terasaki's *Bridge to the Sun*, and William Manchester's *American Caesar* were all excerpted in the *Reader's Digest*; John Marquand's *Stopover Tokyo* appeared in the *Saturday Evening Post* and James Michener's *Sayonara* appeared in *McCall's*. Michihiko Hachiya's *Hiroshima Diary* was excerpted in *Look*, while Courtney Whitney's *MacArthur: His Rendezvous with History* was featured in *Life*; MacArthur's own *Reminiscences* ran in seven issues of *Life* and two of *Reader's Digest*.

But magazines also reveal certain trends in American thought not covered by the best-sellers. Throughout the 1970s and early 1980s, articles in *Time, Newsweek, Business Week,* and *Fortune* explored the increasingly ambivalent American attitudes toward Japanese imports. Magazine and newspaper cartoons are also a revealing barometer of popular concerns.

Out of such disparate sources as cartoons, best-sellers, popular magazine articles, movies, art exhibits, tourist figures, business reports, and export statistics, I have tried to draw a group of themes that I believe have colored American postwar attitudes toward Japan. Of course, I do not think that all of these themes are equally salient at any given time, or that every American is equally susceptible to every theme. But, generally speaking, the next eight chapters summarize what can be gleaned from the floating world of popular stereotypes. A final chapter spells out some of the implications that such American stereotypes and popular attitudes about Japan may hold for future relations between the two countries.

TWO

The Legacy of the War

WHEN ONE REREADS the news stories, books, and novels that came out of the Pacific War, it is not difficult to see why it has had such a strong hold on the American imagination. It began in a highly dramatic, shocking way, with a surprise attack that cost 2,500 American lives, but only 55 Japanese lives. This was followed by a series of painful defeats—MacArthur's retreat from Bataan, the fall of Corregidor, the loss of Wake Island—and some almost equally costly "successes"—the naval battles of the Coral Sea and Midway, and the seesaw battle for Guadalcanal. It was a war against an enemy whom Americans at first underestimated—the "Japs" were thought to be scrawny, near-sighted, and poorly trained and equipped—and whom they soon came to regard as not quite human, endowed with a strange mixture of animal cunning and ability to live in the jungle, and a superhuman devotion to their emperor that led them fearlessly to die in battle or even to commit suicide for him.

It is, of course, natural in the midst of a war to paint the enemy in shades of black and to cheer his losses and mourn one's own. But there was a quality to Americans' feelings about the Japanese that was quite different from their reactions to the Germans. During the early years of the war, the Office of War Information analyzed American films to see how Hollywood was portraying the enemy, as well as what sorts of messages about our own goals were being conveyed. According to a study based on these OWI analyses,

Hollywood had a distinct view of each of the enemies. Germans were gentlemen with whom it was possible to deal as equals. As soldiers they were efficient, disciplined, and patriotic; the bureau was unable to find a scene in which the Germans were morally corrupt or delighted in cruelty. . . . Japanese soldiers were pictured as less military than their German counterparts, and were almost universally cruel and ruthless. Japanese were short, thin, and wore spectacles. They were tough but devoid of scruples. In almost every film showing American-Japanese battles, the enemy broke the rules of civilized warfare.[1]

Some people, notably John Dower, have attributed such differences in the portrayal of the two enemies to American racism. This is an issue that we shall explore further in Chapter 9. But another reason, I think, for the harsh portrayal of the Japanese was American unfamiliarity with and distaste for jungle warfare. This comes through in many of the firsthand accounts of ground fighting in the Pacific, but it is most palpable in Norman Mailer's best-selling war novel, *The Naked and the Dead*. The abiding atmosphere of that book is one of sheer physical misery—the oppressive climate, the brutal terrain, the cruel exertions demanded of the soldiers.

In the first week of the campaign the jungle was easily the General's worst opponent. The division task force had been warned that the forests of Anopopei were formidable, but being told this did not make it easier. Through the densest portions, a man would lose an hour in moving a few hundred feet. In the heart of the forests great trees grew almost a hundred yards high, their lowest limbs sprouting out two hundred feet from the ground. Beneath them, filling the space, grew other trees whose shrubbery hid the giant ones from view. And in the little room left, a choked assortment of vines and ferns, wild banana trees, stunted palms, flowers, brush and shrubs squeezed against each other, raised their burdened leaves to the doubtful light that filtered through, sucking for air and food like snakes at the bottom of a pit. In the deep jungle it was always as dark as the sky before a summer thunderstorm, and no air ever stirred. Everything was damp and rife and hot as though the jungle were an immense collection of oily rags growing hotter and hotter under the dark stifling vaults of a huge warehouse. Heat licked at everything, and the foliage, responding, grew to prodigious sizes. In the depths, in the heat and moisture, it was never silent. The birds cawed, the small animals and occasional snakes rustled and squealed, and beneath it all was a hush, almost palpable, in which could be heard the rapt absorbed sounds of vegetation growing.[2]

In the face of these difficulties, the Japanese seemed almost incidental, as Mailer is often at pains to point out: "The men had not thought about the Japanese at all while they were in the jungle; the denseness of the brush, the cruelty of the river, had absorbed all their attention. The last thing they had considered was an ambush. . . . Once more they forgot about the Japanese, forgot about the patrol, almost forgot about themselves. The only ecstasy they could imagine would be to stop climbing."[3]

And yet the Japanese operated in this territory, and therefore so must the Americans. At times the Japanese seemed to be almost at home in it. John Hersey writes:

In news accounts of the fighting on Bataan I had read about the ingenious ways in which Jap snipers hid themselves in the trees: dressed all in green, hands and faces painted green, foliage caught in headnets and slung from the waist—all made to look exactly like parts of the trees into which they were tied once and for all. . . . Now I comprehended for the first time why the marines had been taking so few prisoners. It was not just that the boys were trigger-happy, as one had boasted. It was not just brutality, not just vindictive remembrance of Pearl Harbor. Here in the jungle a marine killed because he must, or be killed. He stalked the enemy, and the enemy stalked him, as if each were a hunter tracking a bear cat.

And a marine tells Hersey,

They're full of tricks. . . . You'll see that when you go into the jungle after them. They hide up in the trees like wildcats. Sometimes when they attack, they scream like a bunch of terrified cattle in a slaughter house. Other times they come on so quiet they wouldn't scare a snake. One of their favorite tricks is to fire their machine guns off to one side. That starts you shooting. Then they start their main fire under the noise of your own shooting. Sometimes they use fire-crackers as a diversion. Other times they jabber to cover the noise of their men cutting through the underbrush with machetes.

You've probably heard about their using white surrender flags to suck us into traps. We're onto that one now.[4]

Americans learned to fight in the jungle, but this was never their preferred style of battle; years later they had similar difficulties adjusting to guerrilla warfare in Vietnam. In Mailer's novel, the Americans merely muddle through. Despite massive miscalculations on the part of the leadership, petty treacheries by lesser figures, and the total failure of the patrol whose efforts constitute the heart of the novel, the American campaign is won by a fluke. Once defeated, however, the Japanese, too, are cut down to size: "It was discovered from questioning the few prisoners that for over a month the Japanese had been on half rations, and toward the end there had been almost no food at all. A Japanese supply dump had been destroyed by artillery five weeks before, and no one had known it. Their medical facilities had been exhausted. . . . Finally they discovered that the Japanese ammunition had been almost depleted a week before the last attack had begun."[5] During the mopping up operations, thousands of Japanese are killed, and Mailer describes several incidents throughout the novel in which Japanese prisoners are shot out of hand. Yet his tone is one not of moral indignation but of profound pessimism: the war is pointless, he seems to say. In America and Europe it will strengthen right-wing, fascist elements (this is one of the political arguments of the book), and Japan will not change. His most searching comment about Japan is put into the mouth of a Japanese-American translator for the American troops. Wakara (it is his only appearance in the book) was in Japan until he was twelve and remembers the physical beauty of the country. But

behind the beauty it was all bare, with nothing in their lives but toil and abnegation. They were abstract people, who had elaborated an abstract art, and thought in abstractions and spoke in them, devised involuted ceremonies for saying nothing at all, and lived in the most intense fear of their superiors that any people had ever had. And a week ago a battalion of those wistful people had charged to their death with great terrifying screams. Oh, he understood, Wakara thought, why the Americans who had been in Japan hated the Japanese worst of all. Before the war they had been so wistful, so charming; the Americans had picked them up like pets, and were feeling the fury now of having a pet bite them. . . . Well, there was nothing he could do about it. The Americans would march in eventually and after twenty or thirty years the country would probably be the same again, and the people would live in their artistic abstract rut, and begin generating some more juice for another hysterical immolation.[6]

Next to their adeptness at jungle warfare, it was this quality of self-immolation—their apparent readiness to die—that made Japanese seem either sub- or superhuman to Americans. Richard Tregaskis quotes Colonel Edson on the Tulagi campaign:

The Japanese casualties were about 400. Not a single Nip gave up. (One prisoner was taken; he had been dazed by a close mortar burst.) In one of the holes there were seventeen dead Japs, when a man went in to get the radio. But there were still two Nips alive. They hit the man and one other who followed him later. . . . The snipers would lie still until our men passed, then shoot from the rear. . . . In one case there were three Japs cornered. They had one pistol. They fired the pistol until they had three shots left. Then one Jap shot the two others and killed himself.[7]

At the same time, there were plenty of examples during this and other wars of Americans who single-handedly stormed machine-gun nests, who piloted their crippled airplanes directly into targets, or who bravely went down with the ship. *Time* magazine reported that when the *Yorktown* was going down "two carpenter's mates and a petty officer were trapped in a compartment five decks below. The telephones were still working. Somebody called down: 'Do you know what kinda fix you're in?' 'Sure,' they called back, 'We know you can't get us out, but we got a helluva good acey-deucey game goin' down here right now.'"[8] Richard Tregaskis tells of a private who, "knowing he was hit badly, had asked one of his buddies to give him a .45 automatic, and said: 'You guys better move out. I'm done for anyhow. With that automatic, I can get three or four of the bastards before I kick off.'"[9] But somehow when such stories were told about American soldiers they aroused pride and amazement at the men's bravery, whereas when similar accounts were told about the other side, people shook their heads at the men's misguided foolhardiness or fanaticism. It was not until twenty-two years after the end of the war that Walter Lord could write as movingly about the sinking of the *Hiryu* at Midway (Admiral Yamaguchi and Captain Kaku went down with the ship, and as the Rising Sun flag was lowered bugles played the national anthem, *Kimigayo*) as he did about the sinking of the *Yorktown*. And even then, Lord seems to play for cheap laughs the scene in which Ensign Sadanori Kawakami, the young paymaster on the *Hiryu* who was also custodian of the emperor's portrait, made the momentous decision to pack the portrait in his rucksack and transfer it to another ship.

Postwar Accounts of the Pacific War

It is instructive, in looking at American attitudes toward the Pacific War, to compare Walter Lord's two books with each other and with the wartime accounts that preceded them. Lord's narrative technique is very similar to that of reporters such as John Hersey and Richard Tregaskis. Like them, he concentrates on "the little people" in a battle—the privates, sergeants, cooks, and medics. In *Men on Bataan*, John Hersey uses this technique in an almost cloying way. After describing a particularly brave or harrowing American encounter with the enemy, he writes: "I think you ought to meet the private who, when the flames spread, climbed right up on the pile of smoldering, exploding ammunition. He was Harry J. Slagle, from Lancaster, South Carolina."[10] (This litany—"I think you ought to meet"—recurs throughout the book.) Richard Tregaskis, in *Guadalcanal Diary*, simply identifies all his sources in parentheses: "A few minutes later I caught up with the temporary command post in a grove of trees. Major (now Lieutenant Colonel) Bill Phipps (William I. Phipps of Omaha, Nebraska) was riding a captured Jap bicycle up and down a track road which cut through the woods."[11] Obviously, one of the attractions of these books at the time they were first published was to read about the exploits of men whom you might have known back home.

Walter Lord retains the technique of naming as many individual participants as possible, and he tells his story in the breathless, you-are-there style of the wartime correspondents. However, since Lord constructed his narratives from hundreds of interviews with participants, and with the benefit of other written accounts, he is in a sense like a reporter who can be everywhere and know everything at once. What he has lost is the immediacy of the reporter and the reporter's own voice and reactions. Since Lord is writing as a historian, this is of course not a failing, provided there is a substitution of historical judgments for the gut reactions that are no longer present. Unfortunately, Lord's narrative style leaves very little room for such historical assessments.

Walter Lord's greater distance from his subject shows in a variety of ways. Whereas Hersey and Tregaskis refer as freely to "Japs" and "Nips" as the marines they are quoting, Lord always writes about the "Japanese," except when he is quoting someone directly or describing someone's thoughts in the heat of battle. Lord also begins to describe events from both sides, although in *Day of Infamy* only 39 pages out of 218 are devoted to the Japanese end of things. *Incredible Victory* is more even-handed: 105 out of 297 pages deal with the Japanese side of the battle of Midway, and an effort is made to convey the emotions and fears of the Japanese as well as their strategic thinking. No doubt much of this greater even-handedness can be attributed to the passage of time. *Day of Infamy* was published in 1957, *Incredible Victory* ten years later. Not only did the intervening years serve to soften American memories of the war, making more rounded accounts acceptable to readers; they also made it considerably easier for American historians to do the necessary research and interviewing in Japan.

The greatest effort to write a balanced account of Pearl Harbor was made by Gordon Prange, whose *At Dawn We Slept* ultimately appeared on the best-seller list for 19 weeks in 1982, two years after his death. Prange was a naval officer during World War II and served as a historian on MacArthur's staff during the occupation. When he returned to the University of Maryland, where he was a history professor, he brought with him some 450 boxes of documents relating to the Pacific War, which he continued to supplement throughout the 1950s and '60s with interviews with participants on both sides. In October and November 1963, two small segments of his work on Pearl Harbor were published in *Reader's Digest*. These, together with Ladislas Farago's book about how Americans broke the Japanese codes, *The Broken Seal* (1967), formed the basis of the joint Japanese-American film *Tora! Tora! Tora!* that was released in 1970. This film also broke new ground in portraying the Japanese as rational human beings, with all the parts taken by Japanese actors and their lines spoken in Japanese and subtitled for American audiences.

Meanwhile, Prange continued to work on his encyclopedic account until, at the time of his death, it was said to amount to some 3,500 pages. Two of his former students edited these down into the 738-page book that became a best-seller. They have also mined his archives and notes for further posthumous books that have been published over Prange's name: *Miracle at Midway* was briefly on the best-seller list in 1983; *Target Tokyo*, about the Sorge spy ring, was published in 1984; and *Pearl Harbor: The Verdict of History*, rehashing arguments about whether the Americans had prior warning and could have prevented Pearl Harbor, appeared in 1986.[12]

According to his editors, "Prange believed that there were no deliberate villains in the Pearl Harbor story."[13] Certainly, such a view is a far cry from previous accounts that treat the Japanese attack as cowardly and sneaky. Prange instead attempted to describe the emotions, thoughts, and actions of all the major participants on both sides. Here, for example, is how he introduces a crucial meeting between Admiral Yamamoto, who dreamed up the attack on Pearl Harbor, and Vice Admiral Shimizu, who helped execute it: "Yamamoto's fine dark eyes rested thoughtfully on Vice Admiral Mitsumi Shimizu, Commander in Chief of the Sixth Fleet (Submarines). Shimizu was a handsome man of calm and dignified presence. His benevolent smile and friendly eyes revealed a spirit well disposed toward his fellow men. The whole Navy recognized him as an officer of sterling qualities and professional competence."[14]

Prange's editors omitted from *At Dawn We Slept* his lengthy discussion about whether President Roosevelt "wanted and either permitted the attack or deliberately engineered it to bring the United States into World War II by 'the back door.' For the record, Prange dealt with this exhaustively in his original manuscript and reached the conclusion that neither the evidence nor common sense justified this view of the matter."[15] Precisely at the time that *At Dawn We Slept* was on the best-seller list, however, John Toland's *Infamy: Pearl Harbor and Its Aftermath* also became a best-seller by espousing the theory Prange had rejected. Toland, who had written several other books about both Pearl Harbor and the war with Japan, confessed that at first he too "saw no villains nor heroes on either side and could not, above all, believe that President Roosevelt knew ahead of time that a Japanese striking force was approaching Pearl Harbor. Even so, many aspects of Pearl Harbor had troubled me."[16]

Toland's *Infamy* deals exclusively with the American side of Pearl Harbor and the subsequent attempt to investigate the debacle. Ultimately he concludes that Roosevelt did know that Japan was about to attack Pearl Harbor and decided not to warn his fleet commanders. Roosevelt took this calculated risk because, according to Toland, he assumed that the Pacific Fleet would repel the attack, thus crushing Japan with a single blow. At the same time, it would force the United States to declare war on the Axis, of which Japan was a member.

If Prange's book, with its accounts of hopes, goals, and strategies on both sides, can be called the first truly balanced account of Pearl Harbor, then Toland's is most assuredly overbalanced. For he makes it clear that in implicating Roosevelt, he is exonerating the Japanese. In *But Not in Shame* (also briefly on the bestseller list, in 1962), Toland says he concluded "that it had been a largely unprovoked act of Japanese aggression. Nine years later, after considerable research in Japan, I came to the startling conclusion in *The Rising Sun* that Pearl Harbor had been the result of American as well as Japanese miscalculations and mistakes."[17] But at the end of *Infamy*, he argues that if Roosevelt had taken steps to repulse the Japanese at Pearl Harbor, "the war with Japan was one that need never have been fought. . . . Imagine if there had been no war in the East. There would have been no Hiroshima and perhaps no threat of nuclear warfare. Nor would it have been necessary for America to have fought a grueling, unpopular war in Korea and a far more tragic one in Vietnam which weakened the U.S. economy and brought bitter civil conflict."[18] These last two wars would presumably never have occurred because both Korea and Vietnam, like China, would have remained safely under the control of Japan's Greater East Asia Co-Prosperity Sphere. This is a bit like saying that if the Americans had never fought Hitler, eastern Europe might not today be under Russian domination.

It is possible, in surveying the histories of the Pacific War, to detect a trend from placing all blame on the enemy to a greater evenhandedness to, eventually, accounts that blame the United States for provoking the war. Part of this trajectory can no doubt be ascribed to a lessening of war-bred animosities over time. But one does not observe a similar pattern when one turns to personal memoirs and eye-witness stories. To be sure, the painful, searing wartime and immediately postwar best-sellers by participants such as Norman Mailer, John Hersey, and Richard Tregaskis are followed, in the late 1950s, by the memoirs of Gwen Terasaki and "Pappy" Boyington, each in its own way much more understanding of the Japanese side of the conflict. But in 1980—thirty-five years after the end of the war—William Manchester's *Goodbye Darkness* became a best-seller, a book so violent and so anti-Japanese that it seemed almost a throwback to earlier times. And it may be that Manchester, who claims that for years his war experiences were inaccessible to his conscious mind, finally succeeded in tapping into a sealed, and therefore uncontaminated, well of pure misery and bitterness. But if this was merely one man's venting of long-suppressed spleen, the book would hardly have become so popular. Did its publication coincide with a new upsurge of anti-Japanese sentiment in the United States, fueled by the trade imbalance between the two countries? Or did the book assuage an American appetite for violence and machismo, much as the Sylvester Stallone movie *Rambo* did five years later, with the object of the violence (the Japanese in Manchester's book, the Vietnamese in *Rambo*) a matter of indifference? These are questions to which we shall return.

Personal Memoirs

Pappy Boyington was a Marine fighter pilot in the Pacific War, a Congressional Medal of Honor winner, and a Japanese prisoner-of-war for 18 months. Boyington's *Baa Baa Black Sheep* was a surprise best-seller from mid-1958 until well into 1959—a surprise to literary commentators who found the book to be a boozy, ungrammatical account of the adventures of a marine ace full of trite philosophy, and evidently a surprise to Boyington as well, because friends had told him that he was too late with a war book. "I hear it said again and again to me (and I am getting a little weary of the same old disc): But, Boyington, the whole trouble with you is you're so late.'"[19]

Actually, given the fact that Boyington was rather pro-Japanese and anti-Chinese, he probably published his book at precisely the right time. (He also illustrates once again that Americans are not likely to be equally fond of both of these Asian nations.) 1958, not long after the Korean War and before the Sino-Soviet dispute became apparent, was a good year to be anti-Chinese;

but Boyington's animosities go back to some early 1941 flying that he did under Claire Chennault with the American Volunteer Group, which later became the Flying Tigers. While in China, Boyington developed a strong dislike for the Chinese and their leaders:

The informer method, which I found so prevalent out in China, one person getting ahead of another by turning his compatriots in for gold or favor, made me become more and more antisocial as the years went by. . . . Something else became clear. The yellow-skinned bums weren't with the United States against the Japanese. They were all fighting for power within China, standing by for an opportunity to take over. . . . Personally I couldn't see how Chennault figured them. It was so obvious that the Generalissimo was nothing but a front who never said anything on his own or even thought for himself. The Madame did everything. Chiang Kai-shek just seemed to be led around where she wanted him to be led, and, right or wrong, I was positive that the Madame was a number-one con artist if I had ever seen one.[20]

Boyington's more favorable impression of the Japanese stems in part from the fact that as a fighter pilot he dealt with Japanese Zero and bomber pilots on a one-to-one basis; like gladiators, the two groups of fliers had a good deal of respect for each other. After he was shot down and captured, Boyington was often treated badly—he was beaten, questioned at great length, fed poorly, and his wounds were deliberately left untreated—but he always distinguished between "good Japs" and "bad Japs." While he was still on Saipan (before he was transferred to Japan), a Japanese warrant officer came up to him and asked the interpreter who was with him to translate. The interpreter said to Boyington, "I'm not able to translate the exact words, but I will give you the message as best I can. He says he would like to have you know the majority of the Japanese are ashamed of the way you are being treated, but to have faith, because the horrible war shall be over before too long. Then we shall all be friends again.'"[21] Boyington also learned to distinguish between the gung-ho and often brutal military types and some of the more intellectual Japanese whom he met, chiefly as translators. "There was many a college professor, as well as American-educated Japanese, who had been inducted into the movement of Asia for the Asians, with the industrialized nation of Japan on top, of course. Many of this type individual were employed with a reserve military status as interpreters. I believed the majority of them when they said they didn't have a thing to say about the matter. And were in a boat similar to ours [the prisoners']. The Japs didn't trust them, either."[22] He was angry that many of these people were so poorly treated during the occupation's purges, even when he and other prisoners wrote depositions on their behalf.

Toward the end of the war, Boyington and other prisoners worked outside their Yokohama prison helping to clear away the rubble caused by American bombing. Of this experience he writes: "I really got to know the population of Japan quite well. In our daily work of removing the destroyed homes of the Japanese civilians, and even when they had lost members of their families, relatives, or friends, I did not seem to notice any belligerence toward us. I walked by the crowds of civilians, within three or four feet of them, in rags and half starved, and never once did I have any occasion to fear them, before or after the B-29 raids."[23]

A similar picture of wartime Japan was painted by Gwen Terasaki in *Bridge to the Sun* (1957). Mrs. Terasaki was the American-born wife of a Japanese diplomat, and in 1942 she and her husband and child returned to Japan for the duration of the war and the early years of the occupation. She, too, gave Americans one of their first sympathetic pictures of how the average Japanese civilian felt during the war, and of the hardships he endured. As the wife of a liberal and cosmopolitan Japanese (who was in retirement during the war because he was distrusted by the military clique that ran the government), she also tried to convey something of the anguish felt by many highly placed Japanese who did not want, and tried to prevent, a war with the United States.

Time, however, does not always heal old wounds and may, in fact, cause them to fester. William Manchester's *Goodbye Darkness* was published two years after his best-selling and superbly balanced portrait of Douglas MacArthur, *American Caesar*. But *Goodbye Darkness*, which also became a best-seller, is a very different book. One suspects that Manchester wrote it at least in part because he had material left over from *American Caesar*—specifically, accounts of Pacific battles that were in Nimitz's rather than MacArthur's theater of operations: Guadalcanal, Tarawa, Saipan, Guam, Peleliu, Iwo Jima, and Okinawa. Manchester also wanted to explore his personal memories of the Pacific War: he was a twenty-three-year-old Marine sergeant with the Sixth Division who served on Guadalcanal (but after the heavy fighting there had ended) and later fought and was badly wounded on Okinawa. Finally, Manchester decided to combine these two strands with an account of his 1978 return visits to these same Pacific islands—a trip that filled him with irony and bitterness more often than it seemed to console him.

Manchester, like Mailer, bears witness to the brutality of the terrain in which men had to fight. Here is how he describes his first view of Guadalcanal:

I thought of Baudelaire: *fleurs du mal*. It was a vision of beauty, but of evil beauty. Except for occasional patches of shoulder-high kunai grass, the blades of which could lay a man's hand open as quickly as a scalpel, the tropical forest swathed the island. From the APA's deck it looked solid enough to walk on.* In reality the ground—if you could find it—lay a hundred feet below the cloying beauty of the treetops, the cathedrals of banyans, ipils, and eucalyptus. In between were thick, steamy, matted, almost impenetrable screens of cassia, liana vines, and twisted creepers, masked here and there by mangrove swamps and clumps of bamboo. It was like New Guinea, except that on Papua the troops at least had the Kokoda Trail. Here the green fastness was broken only by streams veining the forest, flowing northward into the sea. The forest seemed almost faunal: arrogant, malevolent, cruel; a great toadlike beast, squatting back, thrusting its green paws through ravines toward the shore, sulkily waiting to lunge

---

* APAs were troop disembarkation vessels used in amphibious assaults.

when we were within reach, meanwhile emitting faint whiffs of foul breath, a vile stench of rotting undergrowth and stink lilies.[24]

His descriptions of battles are no less graphic.

There were many agents of death on Tarawa: snipers, machine gunners, artillery shells, mortar bursts, the wire, or drowning as a result of stepping into holes in the coral. As the day wore on [after the Marine landing], the water offshore was a grotesque mass of severed heads, limbs, and torsos. If a body was intact, you could tell which wave it had been in; the freshly killed were limp, with only their scalps and arms visible in the swells, but those who had died in the first hour floated stiffly, like kayaks, showing faces, or pieces of faces. If they had lost all their blood they were marble white, and the stench of their putrefaction soon hung over them. . . .[25]

The deaths on Iwo were extraordinarily violent. There seemed to be no clean wounds; just fragments of corpses. It reminded one battalion medical officer of a Bellevue dissecting room. Often the only way to distinguish between Japanese and Marine dead was by the legs; Marines wore canvas leggings and Nips khaki puttees. Otherwise identification was completely impossible. You tripped over strings of viscera fifteen feet long, over bodies which had been cut in half at the waist. Legs and arms, and heads wearing only necks, lay fifty feet from the closest torsos. As night fell the beachhead reeked with the stench of burning flesh.[26]

Manchester describes the Japanese dying in huge *banzai* charges and shrieking "Maline, you die." After one such charge, "at daybreak nearly a thousand Jap corpses lay on the sandspit. . . . Somehow cadavers always seem smaller than life. The Nips were smaller than we were anyway; their dead looked like dwarfs."[27] Throughout the book Manchester refers to the Japanese as Japs and Nips, just as accounts contemporaneous with the fighting did. It is possible to argue that Manchester's style demands this—that in a hot-blooded, violent book full of Marine argot, the use of "Jap" and "Nip" is only realistic. But one could equally well turn the argument around and say that if the word "Japanese" had been substituted in most of these cases, the book would have become no less factual but more distanced and much cooler in tone.

Even Manchester's 1978 travel encounters with contemporary Japanese are edged with hostility. On Guadalcanal he flinches to see "young Japanese who hadn't even been born when the battle raged here come on economic missions, examining the Solomons' rich mineral deposits. . . . Executives from huge Nipponese conglomerates sit around tables in the hotels, drinking cold Kirin beer and studying maps of the islands." On Saipan he marvels at Japanese honeymoon couples who come to visit the cliffs where thousands of Japanese civilians leapt to their deaths rather than surrender to the Americans. And in Manila he wryly notes that the elevator in the rebuilt Manila Hotel (its predecessor having been destroyed by the Japanese) is made by Mitsubishi.[28]

It might be possible to view Manchester's book as one man's attempt to exorcise his wartime memories, and to attribute its appeal largely to its violence rather than its anti-Japanese sentiments. But four years later, Studs Terkel's *"The Good War"* became a best-seller echoing many of the same sentiments. Terkel's book is an oral history containing many voices, and so its overall tone is less harsh than that of Manchester's memoir. Terkel in fact begins with the recollections of several *nisei* who were interned during much of the war, and he ends with several accounts of the bombing of Hiroshima by *hibakusha* (atomic survivors, consistently misrendered as *hibakisha* by Terkel). Thus the book is framed by stories designed to elicit feelings of guilt among Americans, and many of the intervening memoirs are somewhat sad and puzzled. "World War Two was just an innocent time in America. I was innocent. My parents were innocent. The country was innocent."[29]

But by no means all of Terkel's respondents feel that way, even in the mid-1980s. E. B. (Sledgehammer) Sledge, an ex-Marine who fought at Guadalcanal, remembers:

The Japanese fought by a code they thought was right: *bushido*. The code of the warrior: no surrender. You don't really comprehend it until you get out there and fight people who are faced with an absolutely hopeless situation and will not give up. If you tried to help one of the Japanese, he'd usually detonate a grenade and kill himself as well as you. To be captured was a disgrace. To us, it was impossible, too, because we knew what happened in Bataan. . . . You develop an attitude of no mercy because they had no mercy on us. . . . This hatred toward the Japanese was just a natural feeling that developed elementally. Our attitude toward the Japanese was different than the one we had toward the Germans. My brother who was with the Second Infantry Division in the Battle of the Bulge, wounded three times, said when things were hopeless for the Germans, they surrendered. I have heard many guys who fought in Europe who said the Germans were damn good soldiers. We hated the hell of having to fight 'em. When they surrendered, they were guys just like us. With the Japanese, it was not that way.[30]

Peter Bezich, who served as a medical aide with the infantry in the Philippines, also remains bitter: "Oh yeah, we were fightin' fascism. Kids today don't even know what fascism is. We won the war but we lost the peace. Japan and Germany today, their technology and economy surpasses us. Even to this day, I'm bitter about Japanese and German goods."[31]

And then there is Anton Bilek, who survived the Bataan death march, imprisonment by the Japanese in the Philippines, and ultimately imprisonment near Nagasaki and forced labor in a coal mine. After describing these experiences, he says bluntly, "I'm back home. It's all over with. I'd like to forget it. I had nothin' against the Japanese. But I don't drive a Toyota or own a Sony." As for dropping the atomic bomb on Japan, "We should have dropped [it], yes. If we'd landed there with a force, we'd have killed off more people than were killed by the bomb. All the prisoners of war would have been killed, of course. I doubt if dropping it on an uninhabited place woulda done any good. Not to Japanese people. Maybe another people. They were a hard nut."[32]

The *New York Times*/CBS News opinion poll conducted in mid-July 1985 suggested that age and personal experience strongly affect Americans' attitudes toward Japan's role in World War II. Overall, 27 percent of the Americans questioned said they continued to "hold it against Japan" for the 1941 attack on Pearl Harbor, but this figure rose to 47 percent among those over sixty-five and to 57 percent of those who had fought in the Pacific. It was, of course, members of these latter two groups whom Terkel interviewed for his book. And it may be that the *New York Times* was right when they publicized the results of their poll under the headline, "War Shadow Lifts in U.S.–Japan Ties." But simultaneously with their poll they published another article that sent out a very different message.

This article was written by the veteran journalist Theodore H. White, and one could argue that to some extent he simply exemplified the attitudes of someone over sixty-five. White, who was in China during World War II, also belonged to the category of those who were strongly attracted to China and predisposed to dislike Japan. Nevertheless, his article shocked many readers with its harshness. He begins by recalling the Japanese surrender on Sunday, September 2, 1945, which he witnessed on board the battleship *Missouri*. When the Japanese came aboard, White says, he "bristled at the sight of them. I had seen the Japanese blast and flame Chungqing, the city I had lived in years before, then bring their planes down to machinegun people in the streets. Japanese had shot at me, I had fired at them, and so the luxury of this moment was one I enjoyed." [33]

After rehearsing his bitter memories of the war, White recounts how during the occupation it soon became evident that the United States would have to help Japan rebuild its industries if the country were not to starve or become a constant drain on American resources. In White's grudging words, "It is impossible to blame the Japanese for accepting American mercy and the American invitation to thrive." However, Japan's economy had become so powerful and its balance of trade with the United States so skewed (see Chapter 8) that White felt impelled to warn the Japanese "the superlative execution of their trade tactics may provoke an incalculable reaction—as the Japanese might well remember of the course that ran from Pearl Harbor to the deck of the *U.S.S. Missouri* in Tokyo Bay just 40 years ago."

Thus war memories and war imagery are not necessarily something receding into the distant past; they can be harnessed to up-to-date causes, and White's article was really a clarion call for the United States to engage Japan in a new, trade war. To this end we are repeatedly reminded, as we were both before and during World War II, that the Japanese are aggressive. An unnamed State Department official is quoted by White as saying, "They have no sense of moderation; they are aggressive. They are an island nation looking out on the rest of the world as plunder from a protected bastion." The U.S. "engineering community," according to White, views the Japanese as "brilliant, efficient, aggressive people who prize education as much or more than Americans—and have learned to use it." And White himself believed that "the Japanese provoke American wrath because they are a locked and closed civilization that reciprocates our hushed fear with veiled contempt." [34]

In 1975, when I first wrote about these issues, I hopefully asserted that the bitterness over World War II would die out as the generation that fought in the Pacific passed from the scene. I believed that "the majority of Americans, while still capable of getting excited by a rousing account of Pearl Harbor or the battle of Midway, are no longer very interested in castigating their former enemy." [35] But in 1987 I found myself amazed and disturbed by the renewed virulence of World War II images and stereotypes. The Japanese as a hostile, aggressive, and cold-blooded nation remains a powerful theme in American thought, and Theodore White was right about at least one thing: the Japanese would be foolhardy to discount such sentiments.

THREE

The Legacy of Hiroshima

THE ATTITUDES OF AMERICANS toward the
events of August 6, 1945, are a good deal more ambivalent than
their attitudes toward those of December 7, 1941. One reason, perhaps, is that Americans were the actors in 1945—they
dropped an atomic bomb on Hiroshima—whereas on Pearl Harbor Day they were acted upon. It is always easier to attach an
unambiguous label to someone else's behavior than to one's own.
President Roosevelt's characterization of December 7, 1941, as
"a date which will live in infamy" may have faded somewhat, but
it has certainly not disappeared from the national vocabulary;
whereas attitudes toward Hiroshima have become hedged about
with self-justification, feelings of guilt, and doubt. Was it necessary to drop the bomb? Could the war have been won without
it? Should we have issued a warning or given a demonstration of
the bomb's potential damage? Was it a racist act, something we
would not have done in the war with Germany? Was the dropping of an A-bomb morally justifiable under any circumstances?
Such nagging questions undoubtedly helped soften American attitudes toward Japanese wartime behavior: if they were beastly
during the war, we were beastly too. But, paradoxically, Ameri-

can guilt feelings may also cause us to dislike the Japanese more. We not only tend to avoid people who make us feel guilty, we also tend to "project" our own feelings of guilt, so that the victim becomes transformed into an accuser whom we then hate for accusing us. It is a well-known psychological mechanism in unhappy marriages, and it can equally well color relationships between nations and peoples.

It is important to recall, however, that, just as unhappy marriages may once have been happy, the news of Hiroshima was not initially surrounded by an aura of American guilt. One senses in the news reports a feeling of awe, a definite awareness that we had entered the atomic age, but this is coupled with a steely determination to end the war. In his announcement concerning the bomb, President Truman said: "It was to spare the Japanese people from utter destruction that the ultimatum of July 26 was issued at Potsdam. Their leaders promptly rejected that ultimatum. If they do not now accept our terms, they may expect a rain of ruin from the air the like of which has never been seen on this earth." [1] The following day the *New York Times* reported Curtis LeMay as saying that if the same weapon had been available to the American Air Force as early as February 1943, there would have been no need for the invasion of Europe. The general feeling was that should Japan itself be invaded, the Japanese were prepared to fight to the last man, woman, and child (there had been broadcasts in Japan urging them to do precisely that), and the atomic bomb was intended to shock, or scare, them into surrender. Lieutenant General Leslie R. Groves, head of the Manhattan Project which built the bomb, has argued that his goal was

to bring the war to an end sooner than it would otherwise be ended, and thus to save American lives. We were losing about 250 men a day in the Pacific. The estimated American casualties for landing on Japanese shores were anywhere between 250,000 and 1,000,000 while the Japanese casualties were conservatively estimated to run as high as 10 million. [2]

Colonel Paul W. Tibbets, the pilot of the "Enola Gay" (a B-29 named after his mother), which dropped the bomb on Hiroshima, later said, "I thought it would take five atom bombs to jar the Japanese into quitting."[3]

After a second atomic bomb was dropped on Nagasaki on August 9, the *New York Times* reported that "the Japanese knew now that our atomic bombing of Hiroshima, in which 60 percent of the urban area was wiped out, was no one-shot performance"; and Truman warned, "We shall continue to use it [the atomic bomb] until we completely destroy Japan's power to make war. Only a Japanese surrender will stop us."[4] The next day the headline said: "JAPAN OFFERS TO SURRENDER."

The Initial Reaction

In the months immediately following the surrender, several factual accounts appeared in newspapers and in magazines such as *Life* analyzing the damage inflicted on Hiroshima and Nagasaki. As early as August 20, 1945, *Life* reported a figure of 100,000 dead in Hiroshima, belying later charges that Americans have always tended to minimize the number killed there (63,000–78,000 is usually given as the "American" figure, whereas some Japanese estimates range as high as 240,000).[5] But Americans were more curious about the bomb's secret development and how it had been dropped than about its effect on Japan. In the June 8, 1946, issue of the *Saturday Evening Post*, Colonel Tibbets described in detail how the 509th Composite Group, which he had commanded, was trained to drop an atomic bomb without being told precisely what it was they were being trained to drop. Bombardier accuracy was a great requirement of the mission because "the atom bomb should convince the Japanese that surrender time was now. It wouldn't be overwhelmingly convincing if we fumbled the bomb into an empty rice paddy. To unsell the Japanese on war, the atom bombs had to hit big industrial targets dead center." Tibbets was unreservedly proud of his own crew's accuracy over Hiroshima, and whenever asked

"How do you feel about the mission?" he said he was tempted
to answer with the question "'How do you feel?' We're all living
in the Atomic Age together, and the atom bomb was made and
dropped for the people of the United States."

MGM made two movies about the development and dropping of the A-bomb. The first, called *The Beginning of the End*,
was released on February 20, 1947, and featured such stars as
Brian Donlevy as General Leslie Groves, Hume Cronyn as J. Robert Oppenheimer, and Barry Nelson as Colonel Tibbets. Bosley
Crowther, the *New York Times* movie critic, panned the film because it had created two wholly spurious "love-interest" sub-
plots and because it did not "evince any more than a miniature
span of the full and conglomerate immensity of the subject of
atomic power"; but basically he did not disagree with the approach of the producers of the film, that the development of the
atomic bomb ranks "as one of the greatest 'thrillers' in the an-
nals of man." The second film, entitled *Above and Beyond*, appeared in January 1953 and featured Robert Taylor as Colonel
Tibbets and Eleanor Parker as his wife. It dealt with the training
of the 509th Composite Group in Utah and with the strains that
secrecy imposed on the Tibbets marriage. (Colonel Tibbets was
the only one who knew of the group's future mission, but of
course he could not tell anyone, not even his wife.) Crowther
found this film "tediously long and earnest . . . with the greatest
emotional stimulation in the account of the Hiroshima trip"
with which it ends.

The first eye-witness account of the attack on Hiroshima was
published in the *Saturday Review of Literature* on May 11,
1946, by J. A. Siemes, a German Jesuit priest. On August 6,
1945, Siemes was at the novitiate of the Society of Jesus at
Nagatsuka, a small suburban town about two kilometers from
Hiroshima. He himself was not hurt, but he and his fellow
priests received and cared for many bomb survivors at the novitiate, and he also ventured into Hiroshima on that first day to
help rescue several fellow priests, including Father Kleinsorge,

who was later interviewed and made famous by John Hersey. Siemes describes the terrible damage done by the bomb, but he is also critical of Japanese rescue efforts: "It became clear to us during these days that the Japanese displayed little initiative, preparedness, and organizational skill in preparation for catastrophe. They failed to carry out any rescue work when something could have been saved by a cooperative effort, and fatalistically let the catastrophe take its course." He also notes that although "the Japanese suffered this terrible blow as part of the fortunes of war" and seemed to harbor no feelings of vengeance toward the Americans,

a few days after the atomic bombing, the secretary of the University came to us asserting that the Japanese were ready to destroy San Francisco by means of an equally effective bomb. It is dubious that he himself believed what he told us. He merely wanted to impress upon us foreigners that the Japanese were capable of similar discoveries. . . . The Japanese also intimated that the principle of the new bomb was a Japanese discovery. It was only lack of raw materials, they said, which prevented its construction.

Clearly, this early eye-witness account, although written by a religious man, still treats the Japanese as citizens of a belligerent nation and has not entirely lost the somewhat tough-minded "war-is-war" point of view that even noncombatants adopt during such times.

Hersey's Hiroshima

The account that radically changed American perceptions and feelings about Hiroshima appeared in the August 31, 1946, issue of *The New Yorker*. The author, of course, was John Hersey, then thirty-two years old, who in 1942 had written about "Jap" snipers on Guadalcanal and had approvingly quoted a marine as saying

I wish we were fighting against Germans. They are human beings, like us. Fighting against them must be like an athletic performance—matching your skill against someone you know is good. Germans are misled, but at least they react like men. But the Japs are like animals. Against them you have to learn a whole new set of physical reactions. You have to get used to their animal stubbornness and tenacity. They take to the jungle as if they had been bred there, and like some beasts you never see them until they are dead.[6]

Hersey's *Hiroshima* is not a personal eye-witness account, but a careful reconstruction of the bomb's explosion and its aftermath as it was experienced by six survivors, five Japanese men and women and the German Jesuit priest, Kleinsorge. Hersey used a spare, almost uninflected prose. Charles Poore, the *New York Times* book reviewer, called the result "the quietest, and the best, of all the stories that have been written about the most spectacular explosion in the time of man."

The account made an extraordinary public impact. *The New Yorker* published it *in toto*, devoting an entire issue to the work and banishing from its sidelines all the usual cartoons. The *New York Times* published an editorial on August 30 urging that "every American who has permitted himself to make jokes about atom bombs, or who has come to regard them as just one sensational phenomenon that can now be accepted as part of civilization, like the airplane and the gasoline engine, or who has allowed himself to speculate as to what we might do with them if we were forced into another war, ought to read Mr. Hersey." A number of newspapers reprinted the piece, abiding by Hersey's strictures that the profits be donated to the Red Cross and that the account be published without any cuts. On the evenings of September 8–12, 1946, the American Broadcasting Company cancelled its regular 8:30 to 9 p.m. programming and ran a dramatic reading by professional actors and actresses of Hersey's *Hiroshima*. The Book-of-the-Month Club distributed a hardbound edition free of charge to its subscribers, and another hard-bound edition was on the best-seller list for a month. Since 1946, the account has gone through some seven editions and 56 printings, for a total of approximately five million copies. In August 1985 a new edition was issued. It included a postscript by

Hersey bringing readers up to date on the lives of the people he originally described in the book.

In his *New York Times* review, Charles Poore speculated on the effect Hersey's *Hiroshima* would have on American thought. Letters to *The New Yorker* had run ten-to-one in favor of the piece; and ABC reported that 95 percent of its letters praised the broadcasts and only 5 percent disapproved, the latter usually on the grounds that "the Japs had the bomb coming to them." Poore himself concluded that "nothing that can be said about the book can equal what the book has to say. It speaks for itself, and, in an unforgettable way, for humanity."

It would be more accurate to say that the book does not "speak for itself," and that it is precisely its ambiguous, open quality—the flattened tone, the complete lack of editorial comment by the author—that permitted it to become a best-seller in 1946 and that has since made it a classic. Every reader, every generation of readers, can bring a personal interpretation to Hersey's account. In recent times *Hiroshima* has been read as a stark condemnation of the use of the atomic bomb. Yet in 1946, Charles Poore found that among Hersey's readers "there is very little evidence that many believe we should hesitate to use the bomb if anyone ever made aggressive war on us again."

There is no question, however, but that one immediate as well as long-range effect of the book was to elicit American empathy with the Japanese. The very structure of the account was designed to do that; it is easier to identify with six recognizable individuals than to feel for the plight of faceless thousands. Hersey's *Hiroshima* was the first postwar book that restored to Americans their sense of the Japanese as human beings rather than "the enemy." In the wake of this individuation—the awareness that Japanese had families, jobs, homes, ambitions—there of course came feelings of American guilt; there is an enormous difference between dropping a bomb on an enemy target and dropping a bomb on Miss Toshiko Sasaki, Dr. Masakazu Fujii, and their friends. Much of the same process of individuation was being experienced by the Americans who had been sent to oc- cupy Japan. Again, they were no longer confronting a faceless enemy, but were dealing with men and women who walked and talked, who had problems, and who were, on occasion, quite beautiful and loveable. Both the occupation and the public im- pact of Hersey's *Hiroshima* are responsible for the extraordi- narily rapid dissipation of wartime stereotypes about Japan.

Hersey's book, aside from the fame it brought its author, also brought notoriety to its six real-life characters. Most of them were interviewed again and again by Americans writing about the bomb. Even Robert Jay Lifton, who is sensitive to the issue of "professional survivors," appears to have interviewed four or five out of Hersey's original six.[7] Lifton also reinterviewed sev- eral of the individuals first described by Robert Jungk in his 1961 book, *Children of the Ashes*. Over the years, there devel- oped a sort of trans-Pacific Hiroshima industry—fueled at vari- ous times by American Quakers, pacifists, and leftists, all poking through the same set of ruins. It would be pointless to review here every last product of this industry, primarily because so few had any major national impact comparable to that of Hersey's *Hiroshima*. Only one other American name is indelibly linked to that of Hiroshima: Norman Cousins.

Cousins's Hiroshima

Cousins was editor of the *Saturday Review of Literature* con- tinuously (except for a brief spell in 1972–73) from 1940 until 1977. From 1952 to 1954 he was also president of the United World Federalists; from 1957 to 1963 he was cochairman of the Committee for a Sane Nuclear Policy; and from 1965 to the present he has been a member and one-time president of the World Association of World Federalists. His personal political views long permeated the *Saturday Review*, for which he regu- larly wrote the editorials and, sometimes, major articles. His concern over Hiroshima obviously predated the publication of

Hersey's book, since the *Saturday Review* was the first magazine in America to publish an eye-witness account of the atomic bomb's damage, but Hersey indirectly set into motion many of Cousins's later activities. One of the Hiroshima survivors described in Hersey's book, the Reverend Kiyoshi Tanimoto, took advantage of his new-found celebrity to make several trips to the United States. In late 1948 and early 1949, Tanimoto was on a speaking tour in the United States trying to raise money for a proposed Peace Center in Hiroshima, which he hoped would include not merely the museum, lecture hall, and cenotaph that were eventually built, but also a library and an entire university devoted to the study of peace. In the March 5, 1949, issue of the *Saturday Review*, Cousins published a short article by Tanimoto outlining his ideas and soliciting funds from readers, and Cousins himself appended a note saying that the project was one that "the editors enthusiastically endorse and with which they will associate themselves." Five months later Cousins was in Hiroshima for the first time, attending the August 6 A-bomb commemorative ceremonies and the ground-breaking of the proposed Peace Center.

For the next twenty years the association between Hiroshima and Norman Cousins was close, and it influenced the attitudes of many Americans. Unlike many pacifists who followed in his wake during the 1950s, Cousins was no weeping, guilt-ridden moralist. From the very first, his attitude was one of Christian cheerfulness. In a speech at the 1949 ground-breaking ceremonies (reprinted in the September 3, 1949, *Saturday Review*) he said, "Four years ago this city was a symbol of destruction. Today it is a symbol of hope. . . . The visitor came to Hiroshima expecting to see the end of the world. He found instead the beginning of a better one." He liked the "frontier atmosphere" of Hiroshima; at the same time, he saw that a great deal needed to be done and that Americans could help. He visited an orphanage, and out of that visit, which he described in another *Saturday Review* article on September 17, 1949, grew the idea that Americans might make "moral adoptions" of such orphans by sending monthly or annual donations toward their maintenance. (It was illegal at the time to adopt Japanese orphans and bring them to the United States.) The flood of responsive letters, only a small sampling of them printed in subsequent issues of the *Saturday Review*, eventually led Cousins to establish a committee to help support Hiroshima orphans.

In the April 9, 1955, issue of the *Saturday Review*, Cousins announced his most ambitious project, the Hiroshima Maidens. Cousins explained that on an earlier trip to Hiroshima (by 1955 he had been there on four previous occasions) the Reverend Tanimoto had introduced him to a group of girls badly scarred by radiation burns. Cousins conceived of the idea of bringing them to the United States for plastic surgery. On May 14, 1955, he described for his readers the imminent arrival of twenty-five of these young women in New York, where they would be lodged with various Quaker families and where a team of plastic surgeons would donate their services and Mt. Sinai Hospital make available its facilities free of charge. On October 15, Cousins furnished readers with an "Interim Report on the Maidens," in which he described how their operations were progressing, and in later reports he also described what various of the young women were doing—studying art, typing, nursing, cosmetology—as their scars healed. Like Hersey's *Hiroshima*, Cousins's Hiroshima Maidens aroused extraordinary public interest and empathy because, once again, people were able to focus on individuals.

It is worth speculating, however, on the significance of the fact that all of the burn victims brought to the United States were female. The *New York Times* Asia correspondent Robert Trumbull argued that, "In the case of women, particularly, these afflictions [the burn scars] have tragic social and economic consequences,"[8] but since several of the young women had operations not on their faces but on their hands—to make them usable once again—one wonders whether there were no male Hiroshima victims whose working capacity might have been enhanced by similar operations. It is more likely that females were chosen (perhaps unconsciously by both the Japanese and Cousins) because they would evoke less hostility and more unalloyed empathy on the part of Americans. Men—particularly young men in their late teens and early twenties—might have been too strong a reminder of the soldiers Americans had fought only ten years earlier.

Throughout 1956 Cousins continued to give readers of the *Saturday Review* progress reports on the Hiroshima Maidens, and after the last of them had returned to Japan, he began a sort of annual newsletter in the magazine to keep people informed of the young women's job triumphs, marriages, and babies. (The last reports were always careful to stress that "the child is in perfect health," thereby helping to counteract some of the rumors that Hiroshima survivors were giving birth to genetically defective children.) The warmth and family feeling that suffused Cousins's reports of his return visits with the Hiroshima Maidens struck a note of genuine reconciliation and optimism during the late 1950s, a time when others harping on Hiroshima were becoming increasingly shrill and anti-American in tone. Cousins was not unaware of that trend. In 1955 he commented, "Here and there . . . serious questions are raised about the justification for the dropping of the bomb. These questions are not to be confused with charges of Communist propagandists who have been attempting since the end of the war to whip up public opinion against the U.S. because of the bombing." *

---

* *Saturday Review of Literature*, Aug. 6, 1955, p. 31. Among the charges made during the mid-1950s was the assertion that the American bombing of Hiroshima had been a deliberately racist act against Asians, and that the U.S. would never have dropped an atomic bomb on Germany. Interestingly enough, in 1955 the head of the Manhattan Project, General Leslie R. Groves, revealed that precisely the opposite motivation was at work among some of his scientists. The only group at the project that objected to the use of the bomb, he observed, "did not object until after V-E Day. That group was mostly centered around people who were bitterly anti-German and did not appear to feel the same way toward Japan." *New York Times Magazine*, July 31, 1955, p. 9.

Cousins also gave his readers a lively sense of what the new Hiroshima was all about, and he had the honesty not to romanticize even when this might have suited his temperament and purposes better. In 1949 he was clearly exhilarated by the determined spirit and the rough-and-ready atmosphere of the city. By 1955 he was deeply impressed: "Hiroshima is on the way to becoming one of the most exciting cities, architecturally, in Japan. Already the general outlines are becoming clear. The new park areas have been laid out, the new boulevards are well past the halfway mark, the new and modern civic buildings are being built." By 1970, however, he was a good deal less optimistic:

The hopes for a genuine restructuring of the city crumbled under the weight of too many people, too many things that had to be done in a hurry, too little authority to cope with men who have a compulsion to fill any empty space to overflowing or who think of progress in terms of moving parts. . . . Environmental pollution in Hiroshima is serious and could become critical within a decade.

But even when he was being critical, Cousins continued to demonstrate that his real concern was with the present-day Hiroshima and its citizens rather than with their tragic, but irretrievable, past.[9]

The Anniversary Reaction

Meanwhile, the American preoccupation with the symbolic Hiroshima was kept alive by the ban-the-bomb movement of the late-1950s and the furor surrounding the Bikini H-bomb test of March 1, 1954, when a Japanese fishing boat called the *Lucky Dragon* was dusted with radioactive fallout. The physicist and science writer Ralph Lapp published a book concerning this incident, *The Voyage of the Lucky Dragon*, in late 1957. It was excerpted in *Harper's* magazine in January 1958. August 1955, the tenth anniversary of Hiroshima, was greeted with not only a great many magazine articles, but also the publication of Michihiko Hachiya's *Hiroshima Diary*, another eye-witness account, which was excerpted in *Look* magazine and which, despite having been published by the noncommercial University of North Carolina Press, managed to stay on the best-seller list for nine weeks. In June 1960, Fletcher Knebel and Charles W. Bailey's account of Hiroshima, *No High Ground*, was excerpted in *Look* magazine, and in August 1961, Robert Jungk's *Children of the Ashes* was featured in *Redbook*. August 1965 again saw the usual spate of anniversary articles in major magazines, including the *New York Times Magazine* and *Esquire*.

During the late 1950s there was also a good deal of publicity about Claude Eatherly, the so-called "Hiroshima pilot." Eatherly turned to a life of crime allegedly in order to be punished, thus relieving the pervasive guilt he felt over having dropped the atomic bomb. Eatherly was, of course, not the pilot who dropped the bomb on Hiroshima; he had piloted a weather-reconnaissance plane and was miles away from Hiroshima at the time the bomb was actually dropped. William Bradford Huie, in a book published in 1964, argued rather effectively that Eatherly was more than likely a psychopathic personality who craved the publicity that had surrounded Colonel Tibbets and that his efforts to have himself declared guilt-ridden were simply designed to have him admitted to a VA hospital instead of jail. Nevertheless, Huie's book was by no means a best-seller and had little impact on the Eatherly myth, as Huie himself cynically predicted to Eatherly: "The readers of this book will number in thousands, and many of them will believe I was hired by the militarists to smear you. . . . You became what you *are* because by 1960 most of the human race wanted you to *be* the Hiroshima Pilot." [10] In other words, if there had been no Claude Eatherly, Americans would have invented him—in fact, as Huie demonstrated, *did* invent him—as a symbol of American guilt.

The whole issue of American A-bomb guilt, which few people were prepared to face in 1946 and which was shrilly peddled by leftwing groups during the 1950s, was at last made respectable in 1968, when Robert Jay Lifton published *Death in Life*. The book was widely and impressively reviewed and went on to win the science prize at the National Book Awards in 1969 (the same year that Norman Mailer won the arts and letters prize for his *Armies of the Night*, also an antiwar book). Lifton, a psychiatrist, was interested in the psychological reactions of those individuals who had experienced and survived the dropping of the atomic bomb in either Hiroshima or Nagasaki. (As he reminds his readers, Nagasaki was also bombed but everyone always talks about Hiroshima. The reasons are complex and interesting: Hiroshima was first, Hiroshima was more seriously damaged, and Nagasaki has an old and distinguished identity to fall back on aside from being an A-bombed city.)

Death in Life is a sensitive discussion of some of the problems of being an A-bomb survivor: the "survivor-guilt" over having lived when so many (often members of one's own family) died, the angry reaction to this gnawing guilt and the desire to "close off" the whole experience—to get on with life—and the hypochondria occasioned by the knowledge that radiation can produce illnesses long after the initial exposure. Lifton suggests that many of these survivor reactions can also be found in survivors of Nazi concentration camps or of certain natural disasters, such as earthquakes, floods, or fires, but he goes further to argue that in a sense we are all survivors in the atomic age and are therefore subject to survivor-guilt. Moreover, the desire to close off the experience—a process which Lifton calls "psychic numbing" and claims to have experienced himself as he listened to the stories of survivors—is also said to be a common reaction among the public at large. In his acceptance speech at the National Book Awards, Lifton charged that nuclear weapons had produced "every variety of psychic numbing" to prevent awareness of "their brutalizing effects upon human beings."[11]

Unfortunately, much of this analysis smacks of the old Freudian double-bind: if you admit you feel hostile about your mother, you have problems; if you deny you have such hostile feelings, you are repressing them and have problems anyway. Lifton is convinced that everyone feels guilty about Hiroshima, and those who claim not to feel guilty are suffering from psychic numbing. Yet in 1971, a Louis Harris poll found that 64 percent of a cross-section of Americans still believed that dropping the atomic bomb had been both "necessary and proper." True, this percentage fell to 53 for individuals aged twenty-one to twenty-four, and to 51 for those aged sixteen to twenty; but even these percentages are high for individuals born after 1945 and having no first-hand experience of World War II. In the 1985 *New York Times*/CBS News poll, 55 percent of those questioned disagreed with the statement that the nuclear attacks were morally wrong.

Perhaps one of the men featured in Studs Terkel's *"The Good War"* best summarizes contemporary American views on the subject. Ted Allenby, who was a World War II Marine, then a Navy chaplain, and at the time Terkel interviewed him a columnist for *Gay Life*, a weekly newspaper in Chicago, says:

Right now, I'm totally against war in any form. I say yes, that bomb was a ghastly thing. I was in Hiroshima and I stood at ground zero. I saw deformities that I'd never seen before. I know there are genetic effects that may affect generations of survivors and their children. I'm aware of all this. But I also know that had we landed in Japan, we would have faced greater carnage than Normandy. It would probably have been the most bloody invasion in history. Every Japanese man, woman, and child was ready to defend that land. The only way we took Iwo Jima was because we outnumbered them three to one. Still, they held us at bay as long as they did. We'd had to starve them out, month after month after month. As it was, they were really down to eating grass and bark off trees. So I feel split about Hiroshima. The damn thing probably saved my life.[12]

It may be that as the World War II generation dies off, the number of Americans who believe strongly that the use of the atomic bomb on Japan was "necessary and proper" will continue slowly to decline. But it does not stand to reason that just because this percentage decreases, the percentage of people who feel guilt or remorse over Hiroshima will increase. More likely, the passions, both pro and con, aroused by this event will simply recede with time. No doubt Hiroshima will remain as a symbol

FOUR

The Legacy of the Occupation

LIKE THE DROPPING of an atomic bomb on Hiroshima, the American occupation of Japan from 1945 until 1952 left some Americans with ambivalent feelings. At the conclusion of the bitter war there was very little disagreement over the chief objective of the occupation: "To insure that Japan will not again become a menace to the United States or to the peace and security of the world." [1] But the means to be used to achieve this end became a matter of dispute almost instantaneously.

In 1944, when the war was still by no means over, Joseph Grew, the last prewar U.S. ambassador to Japan, published his diary for the years 1932–42. It was on the best-seller list from June 4 until October 29. Grew undoubtedly had a purpose in mind in publishing this book when he did. He had returned to the United States in August 1942 (in the same exchange of diplomats and nationals that took Gwen Terasaki to Japan), and he had lectured widely throughout the United States on the dangers of underestimating the Japanese war-making machine. At the same time, he had lived in Japan too long and he had worked too hard with Japanese liberals in trying to prevent the war to view all Japanese as fanatical madmen. Aside from the details of the negotiations and maneuverings that preceded Pearl Harbor, what shines through the pages of Grew's diary is a picture of a nation that contained many capable, sensible, and civilized people as well as a clique of militarists bent on war. This was precisely what Grew wanted to convey:

> In the heat and prejudice of war some will deny that there can be any good elements among the Japanese people. Yet those critics, in all likelihood, will not have known personally and directly those Japanese who were bitterly opposed to war with the United States—men who courageously but futilely gave all that was in them and ran the gravest dangers of imprisonment if not of assassination—indeed several were assassinated—in their efforts to stem the tide or, let us say, to halt the tidal wave of insane military megalomania and expansionist ambition. Those people must and will loyally support their leaders in war; those who have to fight must and will fight to the end. But we shall need to know and to weigh all factors in approaching the difficult postwar problems. It is my hope that these intimate, day-to-day records may serve to produce for the future a wider and more helpful picture of those people as people.[2]

Well before the war with Japan had ended, while Grew was first a special assistant to the secretary of state and then director of the Office of Far Eastern Affairs in the State Department, a debate had begun within the American government about how Japan should be treated in defeat. Grew and others who knew Japan well favored the complete destruction of her military might and the forced liberalization of her society, but they did not favor wiping out the entire upper class in Japan—a sort of imposed French Revolution. Those who did favor such a drastic course of action included some who felt extremely bitter toward the Japanese—the *New York Times* journalist Otto Tolischus, for example, who had been imprisoned by the Japanese from the time of Pearl Harbor until he was repatriated along with Grew and others—and some who for ideological reasons wanted to see Japan rebuilt along leftist, socialist lines. In this latter group one might include the scholar T. A. Bisson (who was in China during the late 1920s and may be another example of an American whose affection for the Chinese colored his opinions of the Japanese) and the journalist I. F. Stone. Leftist hopes for Japan ultimately blossomed into a vocal school of criticism of the occupation, but in the days preceding and immediately following the end of the war, the argument centered on the person and institution of the Japanese emperor.

Attitudes Toward the Emperor

Grew (and knowledgeable anthropologists such as Ruth Benedict) favored the retention of the emperor as the symbolic head of the nation. Others, such as Otto Tolischus, argued that the emperor system

is the greatest obstacle to Japanese democracy and the bulwark from behind which the Japanese militarists, industrialists and bureaucrats control the land. Above all, it is the source of Japanese fanaticism and the inspiration for Japan's career of conquest. . . . The simplest way of ending it would be to do away with the Emperor entirely and to see to it that no member of the present dynasty ever ascends the throne.

Tolischus, however, concentrated on the wartime ideals propagated in the name of the emperor, ideals which Tolischus argued were "based on an irrational religious fanaticism coupled with savagery. . . . Shinto is a faith without theology or doctrine, without ethics or morals, without a clear distinction between good or evil."[3] T. A. Bisson had something else in mind when he wrote, "Maintenance of the Emperor will keep the old ruling groups in power and seriously prejudice any possibility of reorganizing Japanese society on a democratic basis." Shortly after the surrender, he further defined this reorganization as "a swift overturn through popular revolt, on every count the safest form of political insurance with respect to postwar Japan. . . . The quintessence of a correct [American] policy toward Japan is to help the people throw out the oligarchy."[4] I. F. Stone attacked Grew as a representative of the wealthy Groton-Harvard aristocracy, whose "contacts were with the upper classes in Japan as those of his British counterpart, Sir Nevile Henderson, were with the upper classes in Germany."[5] Others associated the former ambassador with "British and American tories who declare that the Emperor must be kept in a beaten Japan as a safeguard against Communism."[6]

The average American had no strong opinions one way or the other in this sectarian argument. During the war, Americans had developed a curiosity about Mikadoism—this strange belief that enabled Japanese to fight so fiercely and die so readily. But once the war was over, there was no widespread residual hatred toward the emperor, as there was toward Tojo, Yamashita, and other well-known military figures. On August 11, 1945, when the *New York Times* banner headline read "JAPAN OFFERS TO SURRENDER: U.S. MAY LET EMPEROR REMAIN; MASTER RECONVERSION PLAN SET" (with a smaller headline underneath reading "Truman Is Said to Favor Retention of Hirohito as Spiritual Leader"), there was a smaller story datelined Guam on the lower front page which was headed: "GI's in Pacific Go Wild With Joy; 'Let 'Em Keep Emperor,' They Say." And on an inside page, an analytical article about Hirohito and the nature of Shinto-ism ended by saying "The Emperor is regarded not so much as an active ruler but rather as the source of authority. His advisers exercise this authority and they, not the Emperor, in Japanese eyes are responsible for mistakes. He is, essentially, the passive keystone of the political and social structure of Japan."[7]

The ultimate fate of the emperor was settled by Douglas Mac-Arthur (the "clarification" the Japanese had received prior to agreeing to surrender was not that the emperor's sovereignty would necessarily remain inviolate but merely that it would be subject to the Supreme Commander of the Allied Powers, SCAP). According to Courtney Whitney, MacArthur was under some pressure from the British and the Russians to put Hirohito on trial as a war criminal.

MacArthur stoutly resisted such efforts. Finally, when Washington seemed to be veering toward the British point of view, he advised that he would need at least one million reinforcements should such action be taken. He believed that if the Emperor were indicted as a war criminal, military government would have to be instituted throughout all Japan, and guerrilla warfare might break out. The Emperor's name was stricken off the list.[8]

Subsequent steps to limit the power of the emperor—his specific disavowal of divine status, the constitutional stipulation that he could exercise no political power, and the abolition of the crime of lèse-majesté—were all carried out at MacArthur's behest.

What American doubts may have remained about the essential benignity of the Japanese emperor were laid to rest not by these actions, however, but by the publication of an unusual best-seller: Elizabeth Gray Vining's *Windows for the Crown Prince*. Chock-full of Japanese names that could not possibly have much meaning to an American audience—Katsunoshin Yamanashi, Prince Higashikuni, Grand Chamberlains Shiro Sumikura and Shigeto Hozumi, Grand Steward Yoshitami Matsudaira—this book would probably not draw flies today. But in 1952 it was on the best-seller list for 27 weeks, attesting to the curiosity Americans still had about the Japanese emperor and his family.

In the spring of 1946, the emperor had mentioned to an American delegation of educators that he would like an American tutor for his eldest son, Crown Prince Akihito, specifying only that the tutor should be a woman, "a Christian, but not a fanatic," and not an "old Japan hand." After an informal selection process the choice finally settled on Elizabeth Gray Vining, then a forty-four-year-old widow who had written a number of books for children and who was a devout Quaker. She arrived in Japan in the fall of 1946 and gave English lessons not only to the crown prince but also to several other of the "imperial children" and to the empress herself until the end of 1950. Her book, *Windows for the Crown Prince*, makes strange reading for an American today because it strikes one as both fatuous and presumptuous: Vining involving her entire Japanese household in morning Bible readings, Vining teaching her young charges about William Penn and the Indians so that they would learn about peaceful relationships between people of differing races and countries, about the Olympic Games because of their expressed purpose of "not victory but partnership," and about Pierre Ceresole, "whose Service Civile Internationale offered the moral equivalent of war that William James advocated."[9] Yet she so obviously meant well, had great tact and respect for Japanese culture, and was far less presumptuous in her goals and methods than many participants in the occupation. The great appeal of her book to Americans was the intimate glimpses she provided of the imperial family. She seems to have satisfied her audience so thoroughly on this score that her 1960 sequel, *Return to Japan*—an account of the wedding of the crown prince to a "commoner"—was on the best-seller list only briefly.

Criticism During the Occupation

Other issues over which debates developed during the occupation were the extent to which the bureaucracy, government, and business should be purged of wartime leaders, Japanese industry stripped of its "warmaking potential," and reparations paid to former enemies. During the early days of the occupation, its most vociferous critics were American liberals who did not think MacArthur's purges were thorough enough or his attempts to cripple Japanese industry harsh enough. The journalist Mark Gayn, for example, complained that "the infant days of the Occupation was the time to start lopping off political heads, until we had reformed the whole governing body of Japan. We procrastinated, and with each day of delay the Japanese learned more of our weaknesses, and of the ways of using them to thwart our plans." Gayn also noted with approval Edwin Pauley's suggestion to remove from Japan half her capacity for making machine tools, the equipment of twenty shipyards, and all steel capacity in excess of 2,500,000 tons. And Gayn lamented when he learned that Japan's huge business combines, the *zaibatsu*, were not to be totally destroyed: "The anti-*zaibatsu* laws were to be allowed to wither by default. Labor was expected to 'modify its demands.' Japan was to be permitted to rebuild her merchant marine. No ceiling was to be put on her industrial expansion." [10]

This liberal passion to purify and pauperize Japan was initially shared by more conservative Americans, who wanted to punish the Japanese for starting the war and, not entirely without ulterior motives, by American businessmen who did not want to see Japan re-emerge as a competitive economic power. According to *Fortune* magazine in early 1947, "news and trade papers carried articles by U.S. business leaders denouncing General MacArthur's efforts to rehabilitate the Japanese economy, particularly those parts of it that competed with American manufacturers prior to the war." [11] And the *New York Herald Tribune* of March 16, 1947, reported, "It had been hoped, particularly among textile manufacturers in this country, that Japan would be kept down, if not eliminated, as a competitive factor. Ceramic interests are reported to have raised a $200,000 propaganda fund to prevent the Japanese from 'stealing the bread out of American mouths.'" [12]

But the need to rebuild Japan was compelling: the smashed and leaderless nation was an enormous drain on American funds. In the July 12, 1947, issue of the *Saturday Evening Post*, in an article entitled "Why We're Trading with the Enemy," the case for revitalizing Japan and Germany was made with all the gracelessness and ambivalence typical of the times:

Are we going to foot the subsistence bills of our former enemies at the rate of $725,000,000 a year? Or are we going to revive their economy, so that the Germans and the Japs at least can pay for their own food and other essentials? Washington, though not happy over the necessity for becoming business partners with the gentry who gave us a sample of their humanity at Buchenwald, Malmédy, and Bataan, think it should be the latter. But Washington wants to revive the German and Japanese economies with an American trigger finger on the controls, for it has the feeling that you can't trust those two countries much farther than you can throw a General Pershing tank. [13]

By 1949 the case for making Japan's economy viable was being put more forcefully. In an editorial in the *Saturday Eve-*

ning Post, Helen Mears, who had spent four months in Japan as a member of a labor advisory committee, wrote, "Traditionally Japan has supported around half her population and run her government by profits from foreign trade, overseas enterprises, and services like shipping. Allied policy has destroyed all these sources of income."[14] And in a long, equally pointed article, *Fortune* magazine wrote, "The tale of Japan is quickly told. Most political and social reforms instituted by the Americans are substantial successes; the economic reforms have been massive failures. Industrial recovery in Japan since the war is the lowest in the world, standing now at about 30 percent of the prewar economy." *Fortune* suggested that Japan be opened to American businessmen wanting to buy and sell goods without the constant interference of the Supreme Commander of the Allied Powers. It attacked SCAP for having commandeered all the best hotels and resorts in Japan for its own use, when Japan, "once a tourist mecca," could again earn much-needed foreign exchange through tourism, and it criticized SCAP for its purge of the *zaibatsu* when "the *zaibatsu* alone, of all major groups in Japan, understood U.S. industrial might and were therefore against war with the United States. But the U.S. Army and the young [SCAP] bureaucrats, ignorant of this history, got rid of 2,000 of the top managers and began to work down into the lower echelons."[15]

Stung to the quick, MacArthur—who usually dismissed all criticism of the occupation and himself as the work of Communists—replied to both of these articles, in the case of the *Fortune* piece with a 6,000-word article of his own. *Fortune* had clearly scored a direct hit. In what is perhaps the shrewdest brief assessment of the occupation yet written, it had noted,

What has happened in Japan has been the unexpected marriage of the military mind and the bureaucratic mind; the Army and the New Dealers and socialists who govern Japan, both in Washington and Tokyo, have a natural affinity for the control of their subjects, and other differences have been submerged in the zeal of the two groups to dominate and interfere in the Japanese way of life.[16]

This is certainly not the first time it has been observed that there is a close connection between the authoritarianism of the left and that of the right, but in the context of the American occupation of Japan it goes a long way toward explaining both the occupation itself and the nature of the criticisms that have been leveled against it. MacArthur's men were high-handed; purges were carried out by category, with little regard for what a particular individual might or might not have done to cooperate with the wartime militarists; the Japanese government, the judicial and educational systems, religious institutions, and business enterprises were turned upside down in the name of democracy. One might suppose that once some of the initial bitterness of the war had dissipated, culturally sophisticated Americans would have begun to raise their voices against this root-and-branch approach. And a few of them did. Elizabeth Gray Vining, although she was an admirer of MacArthur and a great believer in his (and her own) mission to democratize Japan, could not help commenting, after she had attended a session of the war crimes trials,

But as I looked at the eleven judges, able, honorable, distinguished men, some of whom were serving at considerable personal sacrifice, I could not escape the fact that they represented only the victorious nations. There was no Japanese among them. There was not even a neutral, no one from Sweden, Switzerland, Spain, Turkey, or any other nation who had stood outside the conflict. Could a court be impartial and justice be served, when the judges were also the prosecution and the outcome of the trial was known from the beginning? Under ordinary circumstances would we consider a trial fair in which the judge and jury were friends and relatives of the murdered man?

And she quoted Justice Roling, from the Netherlands, as saying,

I am afraid to go home. . . . I came here with the Dutch hatred of the Japanese, based on the horrors of war in the Netherlands East Indies and our losses, but after nearly two years I have come to like the Japanese people. They are idealists, and sensitive, and they have something to offer to us westerners, with our emphasis on material things.[17]

But such self-doubt was rare. With the exception of the *Fortune* and *Saturday Evening Post* articles, which were written from the viewpoint of a sort of bluff laissez-faire economics, criticisms of the occupation tended to be more arrogant than the occupation itself. Robert Textor, an avowed anti-Communist who did not want to see the Communist party come to power in Japan, nevertheless argued that "Zaibatsu power must be broken, or democracy in Japan is impossible. . . . It would be folly to put recovery before reform. Even if we did, the Zaibatsu cannot be entrusted with recovery. . . . We should, of course, hope for and work with a democratic middle class. But we should concentrate on the working class."[18] Textor was also upset that under the occupation the American films being imported into Japan were insufficiently propagandistic.

Oklahoma Kid, for example, a film which flouts democratic traditions of decency and justice, was not only widely shown, but ballyhooed. *Rhapsody in Blue*, entertaining though it was, certainly did not carry a sufficiently compelling democratic message to warrant the manner in which it was "premiered" all over western Japan, with local Occupation celebrities as guests of honor.[19]

Textor recommended that Hollywood make more documentaries such as *Freedom to Learn, How Laws Are Made*, and *Why Labor Unions*, for the edification of the Japanese.

Essentially, such a view was no different from MacArthur's assertion that the Japanese, "measured by the standards of modern civilization . . . would be like a boy of 12 as compared with our development of 45 years. Like any tuitionary period, they were susceptible to following new models, new ideas. You can implant basic concepts there. They were still close enough to origin to be elastic and acceptable to new concepts."[20] The arguments that developed during and after the occupation concerned the choice of ideas to be introduced and the methods to be employed in imposing them on the Japanese. About the basic assumption that the Japanese needed radical reformation there was almost no debate at all—particularly since those who tried to question this assumption were promptly branded fascists.

John Gunther's Assessment

And yet the average American knew and cared very little about any of these ideological struggles. Neither Mark Gayn's *Japan Diary* nor Robert Textor's *Failure in Japan* was a best-seller, and aside from the few articles I have mentioned arguing that Japan's economy needed to be set back on its feet, very little was being written about the occupation. When John Gunther arrived in Japan in 1950, he concluded that "before I had been in Tokyo a week I became convinced that the MacArthur story is one of the worst-reported stories in history. By and large, the rank and file of Americans know extremely little about SCAP, its accomplishments and failures, its ambitions, objectives, and ideals."[21] Gunther, of course, intended to rectify this matter, and to a certain extent he did, since his book, *The Riddle of Mac-Arthur*—published at the height of the controversy over Mac-Arthur's dismissal by Truman—was on the best-seller list for 18 weeks. But when Gunther set out to research the book, the war in Korea had not yet begun (it erupted while he was in Japan); and although he added a chapter about Korea and, prophetically, another called "MacArthur, Truman, and Formosa," it was not so much his focus as the focus of his audience that had changed by the time the book appeared.

For by the time Gunther's book was published, the public was less interested in the occupation of Japan than in MacArthur's conduct of the Korean War and in the whys and wherefores of his dismissal, on April 11, 1951, by President Truman. It was already clear in 1950, as Gunther accurately describes in his book, that MacArthur disagreed with the Truman and Acheson policy of fighting a limited war and that he advocated, on occasion publicly, the bombing of Manchuria, the blockading of the

China coast, and the "unleashing of Chiang Kai-shek" to create a diversionary landing in South China. Many Americans agreed with MacArthur that such actions were called for and that fighting a limited war was self-defeating. Unlike American public opinion of the late 1960s, which was strongly opposed to similar U.S. actions aimed at ending the Vietnam war—the mining of Haiphong harbor and the bombing of North Vietnam, for example—in 1951 Truman was reviled for his determination to fight a limited war and MacArthur was hailed as a greatly wronged hero. In the acrimony and heat of the moment—one reporter referred to it as "mass hysteria"—and in view of the bitter debate that developed in Congress about the conduct of the Korean War, it is not surprising that MacArthur's role in the occupation of Japan received very little attention. At most, it was assumed that the occupation was an unblemished success, rendering Truman's abrupt dismissal of MacArthur even more reprehensible. It is also important to bear in mind that on September 8, 1951, the peace treaty with Japan was signed in San Francisco. By the following April the occupation was over, and American interest in and debate over it had become strictly academic.

Nonetheless, Gunther's *The Riddle of MacArthur* remained the only unbiased account of the occupation and of MacArthur to reach a wide audience until William Manchester's *American Caesar* was published 27 years later. (There were, of course, numerous adulatory and self-serving studies, including John Hersey's *Men on Bataan*, the accounts by MacArthur's chief aides, Charles Willoughby and Courtney Whitney, and MacArthur's own *Reminiscences*, all of them also best-sellers.)

Gunther, with his imposing reputation and superb access to important individuals, managed to interview not only MacArthur and his chief assistants in SCAP, but also the emperor and empress of Japan. He clearly liked MacArthur—"What struck me most was his lightness, humor, and give-and-take"—

but this did not prevent him from weighing the general's faults and some of the criticisms leveled against his policies in Japan. Gunther was also impressed with the emperor, whom he sized up as "a personage of powerful will and intelligence, who for good or ill may still play a commanding role in the future of Japan." The emperor told Gunther that he was confident that "[the U.S.'s] democratization of Japan *will* endure after the occupation ends, but that Japanese democracy will be of its own special type, perhaps quite different from that which exists in England or America."[22] This last turns out to be very close to Gunther's own assessment of the occupation. In a sort of wry final catechism, Gunther asks himself a number of questions and then proceeds to answer them:

Has MacArthur done a good job? Of course. *How?* Almost any intelligent dictator can do a good job for a while, given the right material. Simply inspect the record. *Has he done the job he thinks he has done?* Not quite. *Is he sincere in his belief that Japan will become successfully democratized?* Absolutely. He thinks it is democratized already. *Is it?* No. But stupendous progress has been made. *Will it stick?* That is the most important question of all. *Some* of it will stick. . . . A seed has been planted, and something is bound to grow, though we cannot know exactly what. *But on the whole the SCAP record is good, not bad?* Absolutely.[23]

Criticism from the Left

Meanwhile, criticism of the occupation began to appear in the form of academic books, often written by the same individuals who had been involved in the occupation and who had been critical of it then. T. A. Bisson's *Zaibatsu Dissolution in Japan* (1954), for example, is a documented presentation of arguments he was making in 1949 and earlier. A few unbiased books also made their appearance. One of the best was Kazuo Kawai's *Japan's American Interlude* (1960)—a wry and balanced assessment of the occupation by a man in a perfect position to see both sides of the fence. Kawai was a professor of Japanese politics in the United States both before and after the war, but he was born in Japan and spent the war years there, and during the occupation he was editor-in-chief of the *Nippon Times* (today the *Japan Times*), Tokyo's leading English-language daily. In general, however, not many academic studies of any sort dealing with the occupation were forthcoming during the late 1950s and early 1960s.

Only in the late 1960s and early 1970s, did a number of younger scholars begin to take an interest in the American occupation of Japan, but with a pronounced ideological bent. Most of them were activists in the anti–Vietnam War movement and believed not only that the United States was the chief aggressor in that war, but also that American imperialism had caused the war in Korea and produced the twenty-year hiatus in our relations with China. As they saw it,

More than two decades ago the Occupation of Japan set the course for the militarist and anti-popular character of American intervention in Asia. . . . With the seizure of Pacific Island bases and the "reverse course" of the Occupation, the banner of an Asian *Pax Americana* was unfurled. A decade earlier Japan had marched through Asia, bombed Pearl Harbor, and carved out an empire justified by anti-Communist politics and the promise of independence and development. That empire was brought to its knees by a combination of American technology, United States Marine human wave assaults, the fire-bombing of Tokyo, nuclear holocaust in Hiroshima and Nagasaki, and heroic efforts of guerrilla fighters in China and other parts of rural Asia. But the end of European and Japanese colonialism brought neither genuine independence nor autonomous development to the nations of "Free Asia." American military and economic power swept in to fill the void left by the departing colonial powers—achieving for America many of the dreams of empire it had denied a vanquished Japan, its rationale then as now the necessity to crush Communist aggression.[24]

A noteworthy aspect of this passage is its hostility not merely to American actions—the occupation, the fire-bombing of Tokyo, the nuclear bombing of Hiroshima and Nagasaki—but also to Japan and its prewar and wartime policies. (The only people who seem to have behaved splendidly are the heroic guerrilla fighters in China and other parts of rural Asia.) However, such a blanket condemnation of both the United States and Japan tended to create problems for some writers.

For if prewar Japan was a fascist state, could the United States be wholly condemned for fighting World War II? One way, but a very strange way, out of this dilemma was the route chosen by Noam Chomsky. Chomsky concluded that Japan was, in fact, not to blame for its behavior in China during the 1930s, nor for its decision to bomb Pearl Harbor, because it was already a victim of American and European imperialism and was merely trying to defend itself. In other words, the United States was the true aggressor nation: Japan

> was in no position to tolerate a situation in which India, Malaya, Indochina, and the Philippines erected tariff barriers favoring the mother country, and could not survive the deterioration in its very substantial trade with the United States and the sharp decline in China trade. It was, in fact, being suffocated by the American and British and other Western imperial systems, which quickly abandoned their lofty liberal rhetoric as soon as the shoe began to pinch.[25]

Interestingly enough, part of Chomsky's argument concerning the reasons for Japan's aggression in the 1930s is a perfectly acceptable one in academic circles; however, it is usually associated with conservative scholars who argue that America's insistence on unconditional surrender was too moralistic and that the occupation was too punitive. But ideology produces strange bedfellows. Ambassador Joseph Grew, who was reviled by liberals during and after the war as a Japan-lover and a supporter of the "old guard," becomes a hero in Chomsky's eyes for having tried to reach an accommodation with the Japanese in Asia up until the moment of Pearl Harbor.

Another scholar who had great difficulties in reconciling his dislike of the prewar Japanese with his dislike of American occupation policies was Richard H. Minear, the author of *Victors' Justice* (1971). Dedicating his book to "the many Americans whose opposition to the war in Indochina has made them exiles, criminals, or aliens in their own land," Minear made it clear that his attack on the Tokyo war crimes trials was politically motivated: "The war in Indochina changed [me]. For one thing, it soon became obvious from my study of the American involvement there that very little about American policy was right. Could American policy be enlightened regarding Japan when it was so benighted about Vietnam? Very likely not."[26] However, to attack the war-crimes trials as a brand of "victors' justice," chiefly perpetrated by the United States, posed problems for someone who believed that war crimes were being committed in Vietnam. Therefore, Minear backed away from the implications of his study that all war crimes except those covered by the Geneva and The Hague conventions are likely to result in purely political trials. In fact he wanted to see "two American presidents and their civilian and military advisors" held responsible for military policies in Vietnam such as free-fire zones and saturation bombing.

Nor did Minear's conclusions about the Tokyo trials lead him to a completely Chomskyan position concerning the innocence of the people tried:

> The Tokyo tribunal dismissed the claim that the Japanese government had been motivated by considerations of self-defense. It is my contention that considerations of self-defense played an important role. But my brief for Japan's prewar policies stops there. Many Japanese acts on the continent of Asia before and during the war are as repugnant to me as current American acts in Indochina.[27]

What, then, does he think Americans should have done with Japan's militarists? "Perhaps," he concludes, "summary executions might have been preferable"; but then, because this sounds even more lawless than the lawlessness he has been inveighing against, he suggests that perhaps nothing should have been done.

I review these muddled rewritings of history here not because they have had any great influence on American public opinion concerning the occupation of Japan—they have not—but because they do signal an interesting change in American left-wing thought. The early attacks on the occupation share with the later ones a simultaneous distrust of American policy and of the Japanese, who are invariably characterized as devious and authoritarian. But the proposed liberal solution in the early postwar days was *more* American interference—more trust-busting, more purges, more land reform, more draconian measures. Today, in the wake of the Vietnam War, there are often bitter liberal attacks on American policies in the Far East and elsewhere, but there is no proposed solution other than that we should simply "stop interfering" or "get out." As Henry Kissinger observed, this is really a new form of isolationism. "The old isolationism [of the '20s and '30s, primarily a conservative phenomenon] was based on the proposition that we were too good for this world; the new isolationism [is] based on the proposition that we're not good enough for it."[28] During the 1940s, by contrast, Americans managed to feel strongly enough about something called "democracy" to help defeat the Axis powers and to attempt "democratizing" Japan. In retrospect, these goals may not seem quite as selfless and pure as Americans then believed them to be, but it is hardly likely that they were (and are) as black as some would paint them now.

Popular American opinion about the occupation of Japan seems to lean toward some such middle view. On the whole, Americans believe that the occupation brought some much needed democratic changes to postwar Japan, but they never expected to see Japan turned into a carbon copy of the United States; in fact, many tourists now resent that Japan has become so westernized. Once the occupation had ended, most Americans took the rather healthy attitude some parents take toward grown children: we have done what we could; the rest is up to you. If, within a few years of the occupation, Japan had gone either communist or fascist, there doubtless would have been a wave of soul-searching in the United States. Was it our fault? Where did we go wrong? But instead Japan developed one of the

FIVE

The Sexual Nexus

TOWARD THE END of the war, Pappy Boyington, who had been a prisoner of war since January 1944, was chatting with one of the Japanese interpreters in his camp whom he called Jimmy. Boyington asked him,

"How do you think the Americans and Japanese are going to make out when they intermarry after the war's over?" [Jimmy] leaned back on the legs of his chair, placing his feet in anything but true Japanese fashion on top of the table between us, thought awhile, then started talking: "I believe Japanese women would make wonderful mates for the American men, but I don't think that the American women could stand the Japanese men." "Why do you think that way?" And what he told me made sense, and is just exactly the way it turned out after the war. Jimmy said: "The Japanese woman is very affectionate, and is devoted to her husband. Yet she remains in the background, and doesn't try to run everything. But our men, I know, would never be able to keep up with the American women." [1]

One reason, of course, why it worked out in the way Jimmy predicted is that the American occupation brought far more men than women to Japan, so the bulk of the meetings that occurred were between American men and Japanese women. Many Japanese women had lost husbands during the war; all Japanese were desperately poor during the first years after the war; and the

"If it wasn't I ain't fraternizin', I'd want
to know who's he."

army of occupation, far from their own wives and girlfriends, had access to food and other scarce items through the P.X. Thus a variety of motivations brought American men and Japanese women together. The Japanese also made it relatively easy for American men to gain access to certain women. Fearful at first that the occupation army would commit indiscriminate rape, and with a long tradition of maintaining houses of prostitution near their own army bases, the Japanese rapidly set up brothels

"You sure there ain't been no jitterbugging GI's
hanging out around here?"

exclusively for the American GIs. In May 1946, according to
Mark Gayn, there were 668 known brothels in Tokyo alone,
with a total of 8,000 women.[2] The rapidity with which fraternization between Japanese women and occupation soldiers began to occur is also illustrated by two *New York Times* cartoons
dating from September 30, 1945 (see p. 74 and above).

In 1946, there were an estimated 465,000 American soldiers
stationed in Japan to disarm troops and begin the occupation.

This number dwindled rapidly, however, until by 1948 there were only an estimated 125,000 occupation forces. With the outbreak of the Korean War, the numbers increased again, to between 210,000 and 260,000 throughout the early 1950s. Not until 1957 did the numbers of American troops in Japan fall below 100,000. Thereafter, they declined slowly. In 1958, there were 87,000 U.S. troops stationed in Japan and Okinawa; in 1970, the figure was still 81,000, but it dropped to 72,000 in 1971 and to 62,000 in 1972. Since 1975, American troops in Japan have hovered at around 46,000 a year. Adding up all the annual figures and dividing by two (the number of years the average GI spent in Japan), one comes up with an estimate of approximately 2.5 million American men who lived in Japan as members of the armed forces during the first four decades after the war. And this figure does not include civilian members of SCAP, Korean and Vietnamese War troops who were sent to Japan for R and R, or Navy men whose ships called at Japanese ports for shorter or longer periods of time. Nor does it take account of the journalists, businessmen, and students who have come to Japan in recent years, some of whom have also married Japanese citizens.

Given such an influx, it is not surprising that by 1955 an estimated 20,000 American GIs had married Japanese girls, even though such marriages were at first forbidden by MacArthur and were never made easy by the occupation. Japanese statistics indicate that until the mid-1970s, marriages between Japanese and American citizens numbered approximately 1,500 per year, with 97 percent of them consisting of an American groom and a Japanese bride. Since the mid-1970s, however, there has been an overall decline in the number of marriages between Japanese and Americans to about 1,000 per year, and of this number a quarter are now between an American bride and a Japanese groom.[3] Such a statistic perhaps says as much about the growing power and affluence of Japan as do the more commonly cited international trade figures.

Immediately after World War II, it was the American men who had the power and affluence to attract Japanese brides. But what was there about Japanese women that attracted American men so? And what were the effects of such interracial romances and marriages on popular attitudes in the United States toward Japan?

American Men and Japanese Women

The fascination of the Japanese woman for Westerners was, of course, not a new phenomenon. There is a legend that the first American envoy to Japan, Townsend Harris, had a liaison with a beautiful geisha, although less romantic versions of the story maintain she was merely a washerwoman and a prostitute, and Harris, who kept a voluminous journal, never mentions her at all. Lafcadio Hearn, however, married a Japanese woman of a reputable, if destitute, samurai family, and while the marriage did not begin as a romance—Hearn needed someone to cook and care for him, and her family had no better prospects for their daughter given their financial situation—it grew into a true union of East and West. "How sweet the Japanese woman is!" Hearn wrote to his friend and fellow Japanologist, the Englishman Basil Chamberlain. "All the possibilities of the race for goodness seem to be concentrated in her. It shakes one's faith in some Occidental doctrines. If this be the result of suppression and oppression—then these are not altogether bad. On the other hand, how diamond-hard the character of the American woman becomes under the idolatry of which she is the subject." [4] Later, in his book *Japan: An Attempt at Interpretation*, he wrote:

Perhaps no such type of woman will appear again in this world for a hundred thousand years: the conditions of industrial civilization will not admit of her existence. . . . Only a society under extraordinary regulation and regimentation, —a society in which all self-assertion was repressed, and self-sacrifice made a universal obligation, —a society in which personality was clipped like a hedge, permitted to bud and bloom from within, never from without, —in short, only a society founded upon ancestor-worship, could have produced it. . . . Transplanted successfully it cannot be: under a foreign sun its forms revert to something altogether different, its colors fade, its perfume passes away. The Japanese woman can be known only in her own country.[5]

Hearn, like most Western men, was deeply attracted to what he called the "moral charm" of Japanese women—what we today might call their character—but he was not immune to their physical allure. He thought them "slight and dainty, with admirable little hands and feet," and while their eyes and eyelids might seem strange at first,

yet they are often very charming. . . . Even if she cannot be called handsome, according to Western standards, the Japanese woman must be confessed pretty, —pretty like a comely child; and if she is seldom graceful in the Occidental sense, she is at least in all her ways incomparably graceful: her every motion, gesture, or expression being, in its own Oriental manner, a perfect thing.

The same year this was published, Puccini's Lieutenant Benjamin Franklin Pinkerton first began singing about his Cho-Cho-San, "Delicate and fragile as blown glass, in stature, in bearing she resembles some figure on a painted screen, but as, from her background of glossy lacquer, with a sudden movement she frees herself; like a butterfly she flutters and settles with such quiet grace that a madness seizes me to pursue her, even though I might damage her wings." And, as he watches her change from her wedding kimono into something more comfortable: "With squirrel-like movements she shakes the knots loose and undoes them! To think that this little toy is my wife! My wife! But she displays such grace that I am consumed by a fever of sudden desire!"

I cite these early paeans by Westerners to Japanese female charm and beauty to demonstrate that the phenomenon did not originate during the occupation. It is obvious from Hearn's comment about the diamond-hard character of the American woman, that Japanese women with their compliance, gentleness, and obedience have long struck a responsive chord in men who are used to self-assertive, brash, independent American women. But the early postwar years may have heightened this American male response. This was the period of what Betty Friedan has so aptly called "the feminine mystique," when American women were being urged to stay at home having babies and being good housewives. Friedan considers this a bill of goods that was somehow foisted onto gullible women; she does not stop to analyze that powerful social forces may have been at work shaping the needs of both men and women. In all known societies the end of a devastating war brings an upsurge in the birthrate, an expression of both the psychological urge of individuals to forget the ugly fact of death and the social system's need to replenish itself. Men and women want, and society needs, a period of relative quiet in which traditional values can reassert themselves. In the United States (and also in Europe and Japan) the immediate postwar years saw the emergence of a generation of parents—those just entering their twenties as well as those somewhat older who had postponed marriage until after the war—who deeply wanted the peaceful, bourgeois existence that the war had denied them. (They raised a generation of children who, in turn, rebelled against this lifestyle of their parents and sought out the violence of campus revolutions.) American housewives during the late 1940s and early '50s adopted an ethos that both they and their husbands found appealing, but it was not nearly as deeply ingrained in American women as in their Japanese counterparts. When American GIs reached Japan and found women who brought them their slippers, fixed them tea, and drew them a hot bath, all without being asked, they thought they had arrived in a paradise for men.

Michener's *Sayonara*

The best-seller that gave classic expression to all this was James Michener's *Sayonara*. Michener, who himself married a Japanese woman in 1955,* has his novel end unhappily—the narrator, Major Lloyd Gruver, is ultimately separated from his great love, the Takarazuka actress Hana-ogi, and presumably goes back to his American girlfriend, the attractive but somewhat cold and domineering daughter of a general. A secondary romance in the book, beween Private Joe Kelly and his Japanese wife Katsumi, ends even more disastrously when the army refuses him permission to take her back to the United States and they commit double-suicide. Yet the unhappy endings did not detract from the great success of the book, probably because they enabled readers, in a variety of ways, to eat their cake and have it too. Men who had been in Japan could relive their own bittersweet romances with Japanese women but at the same time reaffirm their good sense in having left them behind. For men who had never been to Japan it was a sort of wish-fulfillment book of what it might have been like to love a "golden-skinned beauty." American women—who are cruelly caricatured throughout the book—were instead made to identify with the soft, pliable, beautiful Japanese heroine, and they were subtly invited to learn something from her appealing ways. At the same time, the heroine's reasons for giving up her American lover are enough to please the most fastidious women's liberationist: Hana-ogi is a great dancer who has devoted years to the study of her art, and her dedication to her profession and her audience must come be-

* In the Foreword to Daniel Okimoto's autobiography, *An American in Disguise* (New York and Tokyo: Walker/Weatherhill, 1971), Michener reveals that his Japanese bride—Mari Yoriko Sabusawa—was actually a *nisei* from Colorado who had never seen Japan until he took her there. Nonetheless, he seems to have entertained certain stereotypical expectations, "in that tradition says the Japanese wife is quiet, submissive, and subservient. It took me several years to discover that not one of those adjectives applies, and I am still looking for that clown who wrote the novel about how the Japanese wife allows her husband to be king when he comes home from work" (p. xiv). Please read on for the identity of that clown.

fore her personal happiness. Finally, American women could also identify with Eileen, the general's daughter, who ultimately gets the hero and who, we are left to understand, has become more understanding and less pushy as a result of having witnessed his Japanese affair.*

Michener's portrait of Japanese womanhood is calculated to touch all these bases. The comforting, housewifely ways are primarily depicted in the rather homely Katsumi:

Katsumi was alone, singing to herself as she prepared dinner. I sat on the floor and watched her time-christened movements over the charcoal stoves that Japanese women have used for centuries. For them there were no can openers, no frozen foods. Each item was laboriously prepared by hand and as Katsumi did this ancient work she hummed old songs and it seemed to me that she grew lovelier each day. . . . I could immediately visualize fat little Katsumi Kelly the other night, taking her sore and defeated husband into the bath and knocking the back of his neck and getting him his kimono and quietly reassuring him that her love was more important than whatever Lt. Col. Calhoun Craford had done to him, and I saw runty, sawed-off Joe Kelly coming back to life as a complete man and I had great fear . . . that Eileen Webster would not be able or willing to do that for her man. Oh, she would be glad to storm in and fight it out with Lt. Col. Craford, or she would take a job and help me earn enough so that I could tell Lt. Col. Craford to go to hell, or she could do a million other capable things; but I did not think she could take a wounded man and make him whole, for my mother in thirty years of married life had never once, so far as I knew, done for my father the simple healing act that Katsumi Kelly had done for her man the other night.[6]

The Japanese woman's strength of character is depicted in the beautiful Hana-ogi:

There was a firmness about her mouth when she said this and I was surprised, for I had come to look upon her as the radiant symbol of all that was best in the Japanese woman: the patient accepter, the tender companion, the rich lover, but when Hana-ogi displayed her iron will I reflected that throughout the generations of Japanese women there had also been endlessly upon them this necessity to be firm, not to cry, not to show pain. They had to do a man's work, they had to bear cruel privations, yet they

*However, in the movie version of *Sayonara*, which appeared three years after the novel, the hero Major Gruver *does* marry Hana-ogi, and it is at least implied that

remained the most feminine women in the world. . . . I concluded that no man could comprehend women until he had known the women of Japan with their unbelievable combination of unremitting work, endless suffering and boundless warmth—just as I could never have known even the outlines of love had I not lived in a little house where I sometimes drew back the covers of my bed upon the floor to see there the slim golden body of the perpetual woman.[7]

And, for contrast, we have the American woman:

I looked around me at the faces of my countrywomen. They were hard and angular. They were the faces of women driven by outside forces. They looked like my successful and unhappy mother, or like powerful Mrs. Webster, or like the hurried, bereft faces you see on a city street anywhere in America at four-thirty any afternoon. They were efficient faces, faces well made up, faces showing determination, faces filled with a great unhappiness. They were the faces of women whose men had disappointed them. Possibly these harsh faces in the Osaka P.X. bore an unusual burden, for they were surrounded each day with cruel evidence that many American men preferred the softer, more human face of some Japanese girl like Katsumi Kelly.[8]

Aside from its paeans to Japanese womanhood, Michener's *Sayonara* is also in some respects the first postwar travel guide to Japan. In the course of his story he describes rather accurately the etiquette and pleasures of the Japanese bath; the training and performances of the Takarazuka girls; Japanese foods such as "raw fish and vinegared rice" (although he doesn't yet call it sushi), tempura, and sukiyaki (as well as how to pronounce them correctly); the Osaka puppet theater; woodblock prints; a few elements of the Japanese language, including some very amusing examples of the pidgin Japanese-English used by inter-

---

Eileen consoles herself with (or at least finds herself attracted to) a Japanese man—a kabuki actor. Was this change, in an otherwise very faithful adaptation of Michener's book, dictated merely by Hollywood's desire for a happy ending? Or had public attitudes toward interracial marriages changed that much in the intervening three years? The new ending of course makes mincemeat of Michener's bittersweet title; instead of the hero saying a tearful "Sayonara" to his great love, we have Marlon Brando arm-in-arm with Hana-ogi cheerfully saying to a group of military newspaper reporters, "Tell the General I said 'Sayonara!'"

racial couples; and suicide and its role in Japanese society. A 1950s soldier or tourist in Japan who read nothing else about the country but Michener's *Sayonara* would have gained a sympathetic understanding of Japanese culture from it. Such an understanding was all the more effectively elicited because Michener assumed that many of his readers probably started the book with certain wartime prejudices. Consequently the narrator, Major Lloyd Gruver, is made to share these prejudices at the outset: "I'd been through the place [Japan] and it never impressed me much. Dirty streets, little paper houses, squat men and fat round women. . . . How can our men—good average guys—how can they marry these yellow girls? In '45 I was fighting the Japs. Now my men are marrying them."[9] It is, of course, Gruver's love affair with Hana-ogi that brings about his own conversion, just as thousands of real-life soldiers softened their attitudes toward Japan because they fell in love with Japanese women.

American Women and Japanese Men

If the idealization of Japanese women helped Japan's postwar image, the sexual image of her men produced more contradictory results. To begin with, there was simply not enough contact between Japanese men and American women to produce a comparable effect. Also, most American women in Japan during the immediate postwar years were either in uniform themselves or civilian employees of the occupation, and it is not likely that a man from a defeated country would have dared to make advances to a woman so clearly above him in status. Nor is it likely, had one dared, that his advances would have been accepted; most single American women in occupied Japan were probably there partly in hopes of meeting and marrying an American serviceman. But even if greater opportunities had existed, romantic attachments between Japanese men and American women seem to involve very different stereotypes.

One surprising best-seller of the postwar period (surprising because it was modestly published by a university press) was a sort of female real-life *Sayonara*: Gwen Terasaki's *Bridge to the Sun*. Gwen Terasaki was born Gwen Harold in Johnson City, Tennessee. In 1930, when she was twenty-three, she came to Washington, D.C., to visit her aunt, and at a Japanese embassy reception she met Hidenari [Terry] Terasaki, then private secretary to Japanese Ambassador Debuchi. The young couple fell in love and were married a year later. Terasaki spoke good English (he had studied for a year at Brown University) and was obviously a rather sophisticated Japanese, destined for a career in his country's diplomatic service. Yet his wife was attracted not only by his "western" traits but by his Japanese qualities. When they were still dating, she would occasionally go out with other men although "this made Terry furious. . . . His attitude ranged from wonder to muted rage. I did not stop going out with other men, but I realized that whoever married Terry would have to get her way by indirect means; he was a forceful, dominating person. I felt the magnetism of his dark, intelligent eyes and was a little disturbed." After they were married, "for all his ideas and ebullience of sentiment when we were alone, Terry was not only a true Japanese outwardly but a formal Japanese at that. If he met me on the street, he would remove his hat and say, 'How do you do, my beloved wife.' . . . During all our married life he never once entered my bedroom without knocking." Even toward the end of their 19-year marriage (Terasaki died of a stroke at a relatively young age), his wife noted, "His long years of training still inhibited him from expressing affection in words. Over the years this was changing slowly but something in his formal nature still recoiled at acknowledging emotion."[10]

Obviously, such men have their attractions for certain women, and the type—decisive, somewhat arrogant, perhaps a little cruel—is an exact match for the ideal-type Japanese woman who meekly waits to carry out his every wish. But whereas a compliant Japanese woman can greatly delight even an unassertive man, an arrogant man is not so likely to strike a responsive chord in all women. This may be one reason why the sexual attractions of the Japanese male stereotype are not as highly touted in the United States as those of the female stereotype. Nevertheless, the Japanese male stereotype can exercise a strong fascination on American women, as was made clear when a long panoramic novel called *The Time of the Dragons* hit the best-seller list for 16 weeks in 1958 and also did well as a Literary Guild selection.

Alice Ekert-Rotholz, the author of *The Time of the Dragons*, was an unknown German writer at the time her book was published in the United States in a good translation by Richard and Clara Winston. She had lived in Bangkok from 1939 until 1952, and she set her novel in turbulent prewar and wartime Asia. Her story begins on December 7, 1925, with a party at the home of the Norwegian consul in Shanghai, and ends in the mid-1950s in Paris. Much of the novel revolves around the fortunes of the Norwegian consul's family—he has three daughters, one by a French wife, one by a Norwegian wife, and one by a Chinese mistress—yet the mainspring of the action in the book is a young, well-born Japanese, Baron Akiro Matsubara. The reader first meets Matsubara when he attends Consul Wergeland's party and is insulted by an American businessman.

At that moment of deadly disgrace Akiro . . . developed the Japanese X-ray eye. That penetrating, disillusioned keenness was born of hatred. It was a hatred preserved by a phenomenal memory and by the Japanese principle of education, which held vengeance to be a noble masculine duty. Revenge of an insult was one aspect of *giri*, the duty that every Japanese owes to his family, the state, and the Tenno, the Son of Heaven. As young Baron Matsubara, on his first night abroad, stared at the tactless American, he felt for the first time the fullness of his powers of concentration. Here too was something basically and typically Japanese, an odd peculiarity of that inscrutable nation: that a cruel shock did not make a Japanese cynical or indifferent toward his enemies. It intensified his vitality.[11]

By the 1930s, Baron Matsubara has become a lieutenant, later a major, in the much-feared military police. His wife, whom he despises for not having borne him any sons, commits

suicide to save face. Meanwhile Matsubara is back in China trying to crack a complex spy network, which transmits information about Japanese economic and war installations in China to
the allies. Vivica Wergeland, the Norwegian daughter of the now
dead consul, is an unwitting courier in this spy network and is
arrested by Baron Matsubara, who years before had once met
and admired her mother. Matsubara questions the young girl
and treats her cruelly, but at the same time he is deeply attracted
to her. Finally, when she is almost unconscious,

Matsubara Akiro, who had hitherto overcome erotic tempations with the
aid of Zen discipline, stood before the foreign girl and repeated, "Kino
do'ku, kino do'ku" [which, the author tells us, means "Oh, this poisonous
feeling"]. He whispered more and more shrilly and hastily; the savagery of
the Japanese lover was coming to the fore. He must enjoy this bundle of
glory, sex, and stupidity at once, this very second, so that he would be able
to toss it aside afterward. For after the embrace there came, in due order,
first purifying regret at the loss of masculine force and discipline, then brutal indifference toward the giver of pleasure. The episode ended for the
Japanese man by his returning home to the "pure room," where the last
remnant of unstilled desire was cleared away by the chastening powers of
the mind.[12]

Matsubara does not actually rape the girl, but he comes mighty
close.

During the postwar period Matsubara spends five years in
prison as a war criminal, while Vivica Wergeland marries an
American doctor whom she meets in China. She is still deeply
disturbed by her wartime experiences and somewhat dissatis-
fied with her marriage to the good-hearted but square American,
who is by now stationed in occupied Japan. One day, at the Fujiya
Hotel in the resort town of Miyanoshita, Vivica meets Matsubara
again, recognizes him as her wartime torturer, and yet feels
strangely drawn to him. He invites her to visit his country house
in Karuizawa, and one summer evening after a boring army
party she does so. Matsubara correctly senses why she has come
and shows her into his Japanese tea house, where he is just about

to ravish her—this time, with her consent—when he opens the locket around her neck and sees a picture of her young son.

Major-san's face contorted in a grief that only a Japanese woman would have understood. This package of beauty and timid sensuality had given to another man something Matsubara Akiro had hungered for all his life—a *son*! . . . Separated from Vivica by the greatest of gulfs, Akiro studied the photograph and the inscription and then returned it without a word to the quivering young woman. Vivica was so shaken by passion that she could scarcely breathe. Tears filled her nymph's eyes; with all her might she repressed the insane impulse to throw herself at the feet of this demon lover who unexpectedly burned and froze—to throw herself at his feet and beg for caresses that were like winds in the desert of unfulfilled desire, like poppy petals brushing over shivering skin, like flashes of lightning cutting into the slumber of the senses, like whiplashes, one moment volcanic fire and the next as gentle as the veiled moon and the fragrance of dying flowers. But such raptures were not for a young mother, to whom every man owed only respect and admiration. From one fateful moment to the next the climate in the pure, lovely room had utterly changed. Abruptly a passionate lover had become a Japanese moralist. Matsubara Akiro had not dreamed that this flowery consolation girl, whom he had alternately adored and wished to destroy for years, was already a stroller in the golden garden of motherhood, a dreamer forgetful of her duties. Such a one was no concern of his.[13]

We last see Matsubara in Paris—enjoying once again the scenes of his student days and visiting a gallery where some paintings by Vivica are on display. (It has been made clear throughout the book that despite the Major's cruelty, he is also highly cultivated and artistic.) The final words of the book are:

His passion for her had been a moment of glory between waking and sleeping, between birth and death. Before and afterward there had been only the precisely determined duties laid down by Shintoism and the Japanese family system. Like the Imperial Chrysanthemum, duties were not subject to time's mutability. Matsubara Akiro had been born into this order, and he had no quarrel with it. Tomorrow morning his plane would be leaving for Peiping.

In China, Matsubara hopes to promote trade and restore the fortunes of his *zaibatsu* family.

American Men and Japanese Men

Although by no means great literature, *The Time of the Dragons*, like *Sayonara*, was extremely popular and demonstrates the existence of a stereotype—in this case of the Japanese male demon lover, who is cruel, imperious, quixotic. It is a type destined to appeal to some women, and also to certain men. For although it is seldom noted in scholarly books about Japan, it is an interesting fact that since the war Japan has had a strong attraction for male homosexuals. It is difficult to say precisely why this should be so. The psychologically trained anthropologist George De Vos has suggested it is merely because homosexuality in Japan is less of a taboo and therefore the homosexual is less stigmatized and his life is less compartmentalized. A good many Japanese homosexuals also have stable marriages and children, and their homosexual affairs are treated much as liaisons with bar girls or geisha might be. According to one American homosexual living in Japan, some Japanese wives accept a homosexual lover for their husbands more easily than a relationship with a bar hostess because there is less chance of losing her own position or of having her home broken up.[14]

Homosexuality also has a long history in Japan. As Oliver Statler noted in his best-seller *Japanese Inn*,

love between men was neither new nor uncommon in Japan [at the time it was first commented on by a Dutch traveler in 1691]. . . . Centuries before, it had flourished in the quickly spreading Buddhist temples and monasteries, whose members were forbidden the love of women. . . . Then it had spread to the warrior class, among whom it was frequently proclaimed that love for a woman was an effeminate failing. In both cloister and barracks, the love of man for man was more than mere sensual gratification. Ideally, at least, it was based on a lasting relation of loyalty and devotion. However, as has frequently been chronicled, sex does not always live up to the ideal. The world's oldest profession had its male as well as its female practitioners, and the all-male Kabuki theatre was, for a time, chiefly a showcase for the charms of pretty young men.[15]

The existence, in Japan, of "pretty young men" is no doubt another reason why American homosexuals are attracted to the country. Some homosexuals are drawn to the Baron Matsubara type (as portrayed, for example, in the attraction between the prison camp commandant and David Bowie in the film *Merry Christmas, Mr. Lawrence*). Others prefer the slim, beardless, high-cheekboned, aesthetic-looking youths often found in Japan. The fact that such young men are highly attractive to foreign homosexuals, coupled with the existence in Japan of such "effeminate" arts as flower-arranging and the tea ceremony, which are often practiced by men, has caused some American men to believe that all Japanese males are somehow unmasculine. (This notion may have contributed to the readiness of American soldiers to go after Japanese women: they did not see Japanese men as sexual rivals.)

Like their British counterparts in certain Arab countries, a number of American homosexuals who fell in love with Japan for personal reasons stayed on to become experts on the language and the culture. Some became translators of Japanese poetry and novels, others became experts on Kabuki or *Noh* or the Japanese film. Over the years they have performed an enormously valuable service in introducing traditional Japanese arts and aesthetics to Americans. It is fair to say, however, that in doing so they have been guided by their own tastes and have often emphasized the subtle, the hypersensitive, the perverse, so that many Americans have absorbed vaguely homosexual connotations from Japanese culture.

In general, though, it is the image of Japanese women that was and remains highly favorable among American men. American women found the image of the Japanese woman somewhat appealing during the 1950s, when they were trying to approximate a similar lifestyle themselves. With the birth of the women's liberation movement, however, the image of Japanese womanhood tended to make American women acutely uncomfortable, if not downright furious. Kate Millett, who spent two years in Japan in the early 1960s, began by enjoying her freedom as a foreign woman who could sit up and chat with the men, "until my growing realization that the woman who waited upon me with bowed head was after all my sister began to ruin the taste of my sake and contaminate the flavor of the sashimi."[16] Since then, several American female scholars and journalists have tried to modify the view that Japanese women are necessarily meek and downtrodden—see, for example, Lisa Dalby's *Geisha* (1983), Gail Bernstein's *Haruko's World* (1983), Takie Lebra's *Japanese Women: Constraint and Fulfillment* (1984), and Jane Condon's *A Half Step Behind* (1985). But these studies have not had much impact on the prevailing stereotype.

American women have long been ambivalent toward Japanese men—occasionally seeing in them cruel and masterful demon lovers, but more commonly viewing them as small, rather effeminate creatures. However, this image may be slowly changing, thanks to the growing financial and industrial power of Japan. As Henry Kissinger once boasted, power is the ultimate aphrodisiac, and it may alter the sexual image of even the most prosaic human being. Perhaps the steady increase in the number of American women marrying Japanese men—from 64 in 1965 to 254 in 1985—is an indicator of this growing attraction.

For most American men, the cruel Japanese male stereotype is more likely to derive from wartime imagery or from recent images of Japanese men as hard-driving, cold-eyed businessmen than from "demon lover" fantasies. But the opposite image of Japanese men as delicate and effete probably can be traced to the predilections of the small group of American homosexuals who have conveyed this image in their writings, as well as from the way certain aspects of traditional Japanese culture strike the ordinary American male.

I would not want to claim too much influence for the sexual nexus between American men and Japanese women, but I do think it has colored and lent emotional force to many more visible events. In the immediate postwar period it helped soften the attitudes of Americans toward a country with which they had fought a savage war. It offset the prevailing stereotype that stressed the cruel, unflinching male. The suppression of that warlike image may even have been a psychological necessity for Japan's occupiers. Thus, rather than concentrating on Japanese men, American attention was suddenly focused on the charms of Japanese women, and the martial arts of the nation were played down in favor of such arts as ceramics, painting, architecture, and flower-arranging. Growing American appreciation of these aspects of Japanese culture proved to be an important bridge between the two countries, as well as being of great importance to Japan's economy in the immediate postwar years.

SIX

The Cultural Nexus

AMERICAN MEN fell in love with Japanese women almost from the day the marines landed, but the American infatuation with Japanese culture, particularly with traditional Japanese culture, was a bit slower in developing. In its February 18, 1946, issue, *Life* devoted a page of pictures and text to the Japanese tea ceremony, but its derogatory commentary was a far cry from the praise that would later be lavished on this ancient ritual:

The Japs still preen themselves, as they did 500 years ago, on the studied etiquette with which they serve and drink tea. . . . Perfected at a time when Japan was swept by civil war and was on the threshold of its era of total isolationism [circa 1550], it trained the Japs in introspection, meditation, frugality, restraint and poverty, the isolationist qualities which made Japan the kind of nation it is today.

Oliver Statler, who arrived in Japan during the occupation, tells how the Minaguchi-ya, the setting for his book *Japanese Inn*, was placed on limits for occupationaires, but every faucet in the place was neatly labeled by the American authorities, "This water is unfit for drinking or brushing teeth." American guests were also obliged to bring their own food, partly because MacArthur did not want his men depriving the Japanese of what little food they had, but also because "the Army Medical Department . . . devised a propaganda barrage to convince us that Japanese food, because of the human fertilizer used to grow it, was so unsanitary as to be almost instantly fatal."[1]

Occupationaires no doubt learned *something* about Japanese culture; many men dutifully sent home sets of Noritake china and glass-encased Hakata dolls to their families in the States, but the regulations governing fraternization, the difficulties of travel in a country where Americans could neither read nor speak the language, and the war-shattered state of Japan itself were not conducive to extensive tourism and study. And many soldiers were simply not interested in exploring another dimension of their erstwhile enemy. John Gunther, when he visited Japan in 1950, reported that "one day we went to the Kabuki theater. . . . The theater was jammed; it holds 2,500 people; we were the only Americans there, though the Kabuki is not off limits." He himself added, however, "The Japanese audience moans, howls, and shrieks as the fantastic pantomime proceeds; we thought we were seated among savages."[2]

Zen and Flower-Arranging

Tourism proper and the widespread appreciation of Japanese culture did not begin to blossom until the end of the occupation (April 28, 1952). A bare four months later, *Holiday* magazine ran a long article by James Michener, which issued the invitation:

For the past seven years Americans have occupied Japan as victors. Their occupation has been just and gentle, reflecting credit on each nation; but from now on Americans who visit Japan will do so as guests of a sovereign country. If you are one of the lucky ones, you will find in Japan a land of exquisite beauty and a people dedicated to its cultivation.

Michener's article is a sensitive and sensible tour d'horizon. He describes Tokyo and Kyoto, Japanese foods, the Japanese bath, Japanese manners; he even tells the story of the 47 *rōnin* (also recounted by Lafcadio Hearn and Ruth Benedict, and later by Oliver Statler and countless others). But Michener's chief emphasis is on the artistic aspects of Japanese culture: "No other nation is so profoundly dedicated to art. Mrs. Sato's lunch is a masterpiece. Her daughters' kimonos were designed by skilled artists. Japanese books are the most artistically printed in the world. Japanese gardens are things of rare beauty and even the most ordinary implements of living are apt to be as lovely as Grecian urns." [3]

About the same time as Michener's article, from June until December 1952, Elizabeth Gray Vining's *Windows for the Crown Prince* was on the best-seller list. Although, as we have seen, much of the book's fascination for Americans lay in her intimate acquaintance with the Japanese emperor and his family, she too did her share in promoting Japanese culture. She described her flower-arranging lessons, *gagaku* court music, imperial duck-netting, the temples and gardens of Kyoto, and much more. Both she and Gunther (in his best-seller *The Riddle of MacArthur*, published in 1951) sang the praises of the Tawaraya, a Japanese-style hotel in Kyoto, so that it soon became almost exclusively patronized by Americans, just as Statler's *Japanese Inn* was to make the Minaguchi-ya a fashionable tourist spot during the 1960s.

It was also during the early 1950s that Japan first began to export some of her cultural attractions, partly in order to stimulate tourism. In December 1951, the film *Rashomon* opened in New York after having won the grand prize at the Venice Film Festival the previous autumn. Bosley Crowther, the *New York Times* movie critic, praised its camera work, acting, and "hypnotic power," although he seemed a bit baffled by "an artistic achievement of such distinct and exotic character that it is difficult to estimate it alongside conventional story films." [4] *Ugetsu*, which he reviewed on September 8, 1954, after its New York premiere, he also judged "hard for American audiences to comprehend . . . for both the theme and the style of exposition . . . have a strangely obscure, inferential, almost studiedly perplexing quality." [5] But Crowther was completely won over by the beautiful *Gate of Hell*, which won the Cannes Film Festival's grand prize in the spring of 1954 and made its appearance in New York in December of that year. He not only praised its color—"of a richness and harmony that matches that of any film we've ever seen"—but was caught up by its story and atmosphere. "It is hard to convey in simple language the moving qualities of this lovely film. . . . The secret, perhaps, of its rare excitement is the subtlety with which it blends a subterranean flood of hot emotions with the most magnificent flow of surface serenity. . . . The very essence of ancient Japanese culture is rendered a tangible stimulant in this film." [6] Consul General Jun Tsuchiya, who attended and spoke at the New York opening of *Gate of Hell*, took a more practical line: "To me, it is entirely conceivable that the export of superior films will greatly help my country in its present unremitting struggle to become self-sufficient, to rely on trade, not aid." He said he expected that the export of such films would also stimulate tourism and travel to Japan. [7]

In addition to Japanese films, the year 1954 brought New Yorkers the Azuma Kabuki Dancers—the first time live Kabuki had been seen in the United States—and a replica of a sixteenth-century Japanese house (a "gift of the Japanese people") on view in the garden of the Museum of Modern Art. The Azuma Kabuki group became a New York sellout attraction and occasioned a cover article in the *Saturday Review of Literature* by the Kabuki scholar Faubion Bowers. Actually, the Kabuki seen in New York was not wholly traditional since Azuma, the group's founder and the daughter of a famous Kabuki actor, took the major female roles herself. In traditional Kabuki, all female roles are enacted by men. Bowers was careful to explain that these female impersonators, "while leading ordinary conventional lives, playing baseball, and rearing large families, are often idolized by their fans for their exquisite onstage femininity." [8] Nevertheless, Sol Hurok may have judged 1954 America insufficiently prepared to absorb both the strange conventions of Kabuki and the sight of men in drag. Even without the element of men portraying women, the *New York Times* reviewer John Martin—who raved about the costumes, music, acting, and dancing—noted that, "though there is assuredly no lack of vigor, everything is characterized by delicacy and proportion."[9]

The Japanese house at the Museum of Modern Art was praised in almost identical terms. The Sunday *New York Times Magazine* devoted several pages of commentary and photos to the house on the day of its opening to the public, June 20, 1954, particularly noting that "the empty rooms have a luxury of space and an uncluttered serenity." This led one reader to write in that, while she admired the restful, "uncluttered look," she wondered whether life was not of its very nature full of clutter, prompting yet another New Yorker to respond:

A Huzzah! for Mrs. Helen Gross for her letter . . . and a resounding boo for all those who scream with delight over that "uncluttered" Japanese house at the Museum of Modern Art. I . . . spent an uncomfortable time last winter dining and sleeping in a Japanese inn that was just as uncluttered and unlivable. . . . I suggest some of your uncluttered, airy readers and writers try sleeping on the floor in an uncluttered, drafty room in a 20-degree January night.[10]

Clearly, not everyone was instantaneously captivated by Japanese housing, although the *New York Times Magazine* was no doubt correct in pointing out that "despite its exotic, far-away quality, the house has . . . a unique relevance to modern Western architecture. The flexible, open plan, the closely related indoor and outdoor areas, the structural elements emphasized as decorative, are all devices common to our own architecture today."

Still another cultural export of Japan during the mid-1950s was Zen Buddhism. In one sense, it is probably accurate to say that Zen had a rather limited appeal—primarily on college campuses, which a decade later turned to drugs and Indian mysticism, and among members of the Beat Generation such as Jack Kerouac, Allen Ginsberg, and Gary Snyder. But Zen philosophy also influenced the later work of J. D. Salinger—for example, his two stories "Franny" and "Zooey," which first appeared in *The*

New Yorker in 1955 and 1957, and which went on to become a best-selling book in 1961. And Zen had two indefatigable popularizers who became known to the general public, Daisetz Suzuki and Alan Watts. Suzuki, who was Japanese-born but was then living and lecturing in the United States, was the subject of a highly flattering profile in the August 31, 1957, issue of *The New Yorker*. Elizabeth Gray Vining, who had first met him in 1947 in Japan, devoted a chapter of her 1960 book, *Return to Japan*, to Suzuki and Zen, in which she wrote about him: "One knew at once that he had had the experience called *satori*, that breaking through the mind barrier into the wholeness of understanding which is the goal of the Zen devotee. Light and love seemed to stream from him; his gentleness was clothed in simplicity, his austerity touched with humor."[11] Alan Watts, meanwhile, was lecturing about Zen on television and radio, as well as writing some two dozen books to explain Zen to Americans. Watts was canonized in the April 21, 1961, issue of *Life*, which devoted four pages of text and photos to him and his works.

The Return of the Samurai

It was not until the late 1950s, a full decade after the end of World War II, that the more martial, less delicate aspects of Japanese culture reappeared on U.S. movie screens. In 1956, Kurosawa's film *The Seven Samurai* was first shown in New York. Bosley Crowther compared it to *High Noon*, an apt observation since in 1960 the Japanese film was actually remade as an American western, with gun-slingers replacing the samurai who saved farmers from the depredations of bandits. The year 1957 also brought Americans a return of Mr. Moto, John Marquand's Japanese detective. In 1934, Marquand had published his first Mr. Moto story (the novel *No Hero*, published first in the *Saturday Evening Post* as "Mr. Moto Takes a Hand") after a trip to the Far East to collect local color. Between then and the outbreak of war, Marquand published five more Mr. Moto novels, the last of them (*Last Laugh, Mr. Moto*) serialized in *Collier's* only three months before Pearl Harbor.

Just as the prewar Mr. Moto stories had darkened to conform with the troubled times, so the first postwar novel, *Stopover Tokyo*, paints a rather accurate picture of postoccupation Japan, which Marquand had revisited in 1955, and of American attitudes. The American hero works for the CIA, and the villains are the Russians (or "Commies") who have trained several Americans to work in Japan as spies. These Russian-trained spies are plotting to kill a liberal Japanese politician and pin it on the Americans, thereby hoping to provoke anti-American riots. The ultimate aim of the villains is to move Japan into the Communist camp. As the American CIA chief says to the hero, "Frankly, I wouldn't say that Japan is very firmly in the camp of the freedom-loving nations. Why should it be? Well, we lost China, and God help us if Japan goes Communist. We'll be in the grinders then." Says Mr. Moto to the hero, "I am being frank. . . . There are groups here on the Left, and on the Right, too, so anxious to arouse feelings against America. And the plain Japanese man can change so quickly." *Stopover Tokyo* has a gloomy, cold war atmosphere, not unlike that of *The Spy Who Came in from the Cold*; spies kill each other quietly so that the average citizen can sleep a little more safely in his bed. Mr. Moto and his American counterpart are professionals who can joke about their wartime work, which made them temporary enemies: "'In Burma, Mr. Rhyce . . . we had your name on file. Japanese linguist, born in Japan. I even had a glimpse of you once at Myitkyna.' Mr. Moto laughed heartily. 'I did not speak because I was moving the other way.'"[12]

Marquand caught a political mood and invented a plot for it that a few years later was transmuted into reality: In October 1960, the socialist leader Asanuma was stabbed to death by a right-wing student; earlier that year riots over the renegotiation of the Japanese-American Security Treaty had led to the cancellation of a planned visit to Japan by President Eisenhower.

Americans were temporarily shocked and dismayed by these events, just as they were a decade later by the grisly ritual suicide of Yukio Mishima. Newspapers worried anew over the Japanese penchant for violence and fanaticism and speculated about the relative strengths of the militant political left and right. But basically, these events had a short half-life in America's consciousness. Six months after John F. Kennedy was elected President, Edwin O. Reischauer arrived in Japan as the new U.S. ambassador, vowing to reopen "the broken dialogue with Japan"; he implied that problems between the two countries were as much America's fault as Japan's and pledged himself to improve "understanding" between the two nations. Even apart from Reischauer's efforts, the cold war was loosening its grip on American thinking and there was a growing sense that Japan had to be judged on its own terms and not merely as a former protégé. The change in American outlook is palpable if one compares, for example, Elizabeth Gray Vining's *Windows for the Crown Prince*, published in 1952, with her *Return to Japan*, published in 1960. Whereas in the first book she often sounds sanctimonious and full of talk about the need to imbue the Japanese people (and particularly Crown Prince Akihito) with the values of democracy and individualism, her second book is much more that of someone enjoying and trying to understand the Japaneseness of Japan. It is the book not of a teacher, but of a tourist.

Tourism and Japanese Inns

The decade of the 1960s truly launched American tourism to Japan (see Table 2). In 1961 the number of American visitors for the first time passed 100,000 a year, and by 1970 it had passed 300,000. The period embraced, in 1964, the first Olympics to be held in Japan (or in any Asian country, for that matter), and, in 1970, the first Japanese-based world's fair. Japan presented an extraordinarily attractive visage to foreigners during this decade. The grinding hardships of the immediate postwar years were over,

TABLE 2

American Visitors to Japan (Tourists, Students, and Businessmen)

Year	Number of visitors	Year	Number of visitors
1951	6,600	1971	271,029
1952	13,746	1972	315,897
1953	18,154	1973	249,012
1954	23,157	1974	210,690
1955	28,194	1975	241,065
1956	35,593	1976	277,519
1957	41,041	1977	306,499
1958	53,924	1978	278,394
1959	71,585	1979	259,086
1960	85,881	1980	279,416
1961	103,150	1981	311,755
1962	114,497	1982	353,679
1963	129,814	1983	400,456
1964	136,446	1984	435,754
1965	150,200	1985	487,713
1966	173,500	1986	c. 480,000
1967	187,373		
1968	199,581		
1969	255,663		
1970	315,211		

SOURCE: Government of Japan, Ministry of Transportation (Tourist Industry Bureau) and Ministry of Justice. There is no single series of tourism figures for all of these years, but where there were discrepancies the lower figure was chosen.

NOTE: In-transit visitors are not included.

and life was becoming somewhat more comfortable—particularly for the tourist taking advantage of a favorable exchange rate. Japan was rapidly becoming a modern, industrialized nation, but not so rapidly that the old culture could not still be seen and savored. It was, in short, a perfect time to visit Zen temples and gardens, to buy lacquerware and mingei pottery, and also to travel in brand-new "bullet" trains and air-conditioned taxis, and buy cameras and watches. In October 1961, when *Holiday* magazine devoted an entire issue to Japan, it stressed precisely this exotic and appealing mixture of old and new. The editors noted, "Of all the countries to which *Holiday* has devoted special issues, none has been more difficult to understand, more demanding of patience, than Japan. It *is* remote from our comprehension, it *is* baffling, it *is* topsy-turvy to the eye and mind. Japan presents us with an overwhelming double image, one face turned to its classical past, the other preoccupied with the present and with Western ways of thinking, behaving, working." Unfortunately, some people seemed to expect that this double image would persist unchanged forever. But just as it has cynically been said that in the United States an integrated neighborhood is merely one in transit between being all-white and be-

"Well, anyway, it keeps the rain out."

Drawing by Dick Oldden. Reprinted by permission.

Drawing by Dick Oldden. Reprinted by permission.

coming all-black, so one suspects that Japan during the 1960s was in transit between being a still partly traditional Asian nation and becoming a fully westernized world power. And the more Japan moved in the latter direction, the less most tourists liked it.

Four cartoons published in the October 21, 1969, issue of *Look* magazine illustrate some of the ambivalent feelings of Americans toward Japan during the 1960s (see pp. 102–5). The

"Someday, son, all this will be yours."

Drawing by Dick Oldden. Reprinted by permission.

cartoons comment on the crass response of American tourists to Japanese architecture, on the Japanese student riots of the 1960s, on the cramped living conditions in Japan, and on the strange mixture of old and new in the culture. By contrast, a cartoon dating from the mid-1970s (see p. 106) shows that Japanese movies were no longer an incomprehensible or avant-garde art form

Drawing by Dick Oldden. Reprinted by permission.

in the United States, but something that had filtered down to a large segment of the population. And a popular cartoon strip dating from 1985 (see p. 107) demonstrates that by then Japanese raw fish and vinegared rice had also become well-known and liked in the United States. (When I asked 1985 college students what words they associated with Japan, 20 percent came up with "*sushi*," whereas in 1973 no one mentioned this word.)

A plethora of tourist-oriented books about Japan was published during the 1960s; for a while it seemed as if everyone who had been there for even a brief period of time (David Riesman's voluminous *Conversations in Japan* is based on a two-month visit) wanted to tell the world about it. The books ranged from

*I'll go to a Japanese movie with you only if you promise
you won't do that awful samurai grunting after.*

© 1985 United Feature Syndicate, Inc.

the arty (Fosco Maraini's *Meeting with Japan*, Sacheverell Sit-well's *The Bridge of the Brocade Sash*) to the journalistic (Alexander Campbell's *The Heart of Japan*, Richard Halloran, *Japan: Images and Realities*) to the philosophical (Arthur Koestler's *The Lotus and the Robot*) to the unclassifiable (my personal favorite for this period, Bernard Rudofsky's *The Kimono Mind*). But none of these books was an American best-seller (although Maraini's book came close). The one book that was a best-seller for half a year in 1961 and that continued to sell to tourists going to Japan in subsequent years was Oliver Statler's *Japanese Inn*.

One is tempted to call *Japanese Inn* a "deserved" best-seller because it is a well-researched, intelligently conceived, and charmingly executed book that still reads well today. At the same time, it is doubtful that it would be a best seller if it were published today, and Statler has written other, equally good books about Japan since 1961 that have disappeared without a trace. *Japanese Inn* was obviously timely. It coincided with the American general public's curiosity about Japan and the tourists' desire to read something about Japan before they went there. *Japanese Inn* satisfied both these audiences because it was not a pure travelogue—a recitation of cities, scenes, and impressions that is more likely to interest someone who is actually going to these places than the armchair traveler. Instead, *Japanese Inn* is a form of "potted history"—a fictionalized treatment of historical events and cultural developments, set in an actual inn. Statler is frank to admit that most of the connections between the inn and the historical figures in his book are invented: "The account of the inn's founding conforms to family legend, but most of the links with historical personalities, all of whom I have tried to present faithfully, are my own invention. This is true up until the time of Prince Saionji: Saionji's relationship to the inn is given as it was."[13] But spurious or not, *Japanese Inn* did not ill serve the thousands of American tourists who spent a pleasant night or two at the Minaguchi-ya dreaming of the shoguns and samurai who had preceded them. It merely catered to and reinforced their more romantic perceptions of Japan.

James Bond in Japan

Three years later, a slightly different but equally exotic vision of Japan was captivating many Americans. Ian Fleming's *You Only Live Twice* is full of shrewd observations about Japan, but inevitably, given its genre, it stresses the elements of violence in the culture. James Bond's archenemy, Ernst Blofeld, has moved to Japan and bought a medieval castle, which he has landscaped with poisonous plants, piranha-filled pools, and dangerous sulfur springs. The purpose is to lure the supposedly suicide-prone Japanese to their deaths: "A garden that would be like a deadly fly-trap for human beings, a killing bottle for those who wanted to die. And of course Japan, with the highest suicide statistics in the world, a country with an unquenchable thirst for the bizarre, the cruel, and the terrible, would provide the perfect last refuge for [Blofeld]."[14] In order to kill Blofeld, Bond is given a short course in *ninjutsu* by his Japanese police contact, Tiger Tanaka (who had hoped to be a kamikaze pilot during the war):

My agents are trained in one of the arts most dreaded in Japan—*ninjutsu*, which is, literally, the art of stealth or invisibility. All the men you will see have already graduated in at least ten of the eighteen martial arts of *bushido*, or "way of the warrior," and they are now learning to be *ninja*, or "stealers-in," which has for centuries been part of the basic training of spies and assassins and saboteurs.[15]

At the same time, Fleming puts down some of the treasured peaceful arts of Japan:

The geisha party had been going on for two hours, and Bond's jaws were aching with the unending smiles and polite repartee. Far from being entertained by the geisha, or bewitched by the inscrutable discords issuing from the catskin-covered box of the three-stringed *samisen*, Bond had found himself having to try desperately to make the party go. . . . Dikko Henderson had warned him that geisha parties were more or less the equivalent, for a foreigner, of trying to entertain a lot of unknown children in a nursery with a strict governess, the madame looking on.[16]

It all seems a far cry from Michener's *Sayonara* until one meets Bond's abalone-diving girlfriend Kissy Suzuki and we are once again face to face with the perfect Japanese woman: loyal, brave, selfless.

If one were to try to generalize about popular American impressions of Japanese culture from Michener to Fleming—that is, from 1954 to 1964—there would be a number of constants: the charm of Japanese women, the beauty of the landscape, and the refinement of many of the traditional arts. One would also have to note some changes. There seemed to be a progression in American interest from some of the more obvious features of traditional Japanese culture (flower-arranging, Kabuki, woodblock prints) to some of the more subtle aspects (Zen, mingei pottery, Japanese gardens) to, finally, a renewed interest in some of its more martial aspects (akido and kendo, samurai movies, ritual suicide). A social psychologist might argue that such a progression of images was, in fact, a rather salutary sign of an increasing American ability to come to terms with Japanese culture in all its dimensions. In the immediate postwar years Americans may have feminized Japanese society partly because they wanted to repress their wartime memories. They were aided in their efforts by the fact that they came as conquerors and Japanese men tried to keep a low profile. Only slowly did a more masculine image of Japan begin to re-emerge, both in American depictions of the traditional culture and in attitudes toward its newly assertive businessmen.

Perhaps by 1975 Americans were psychologically ready to embrace a new best-selling novel that would cater to *all* their stereotypical images of Japan: violent as well as artistic, negative as well as positive. This novel was, of course, James Clavell's enormously popular *Shōgun*. The book and the 12-hour television drama made from it probably reached more people than all the best-sellers on Japan of the preceding thirty years put together. It is therefore a matter of some importance exactly what sort of impressions Americans may have formed, or had reinforced, by Clavell's work and by two subsequent "coat-tail" best-sellers—*The Ninja* and *The Miko*—by Eric Van Lustbader.

SEVEN

Of Shoguns and Ninjas

IN THE SUMMER OF 1975, James Clavell's *Shō-gun* burst upon the American literary scene. It was on the best-seller list for 32 weeks and went on to sell some 7 million copies in paperback over the next five years. Then, on September 15–19, 1980, a six-part, 12-hour television adaptation was shown on NBC during the prime evening hours. The network, as well as various university groups, put out teaching aids to guide students who were discussing the series in their classes. And Dell Publishing Company printed another 3.5 million copies of the novel. Five years later the book was still in print and a two-hour version of the television drama was available for showing on home videotape players.

Unlike many best-selling novels that are panned by the critics, *Shōgun* was well-reviewed. Webster Schott wrote in the *New York Times Book Review* that "Clavell has a gift. . . . He breathes narrative. It's almost impossible not to continue to read *Shōgun* once having opened it."[1] And indeed, despite its enormous length (802 pages in hardback; 1210 in paperback), the novel has great narrative drive: Clavell writes splendidly about the sea, shipwrecks, battles, and political confrontations. There is also much violence: heads get chopped off by arrogant samurai, disloyal retainers are ordered to commit *seppuku* (ritual suicide), and enemies are boiled alive in iron cauldrons.

Given the book's aura of violence, it is probably not coincidental that as a young man James Clavell spent World War II in Changi, a Japanese prisoner-of-war camp in Singapore (described in his first novel, *King Rat*). Clavell has claimed repeatedly in print that he does not hate the Japanese but in fact admires them: "It's possible to end up admiring an enemy. The relationship of conqueror and conquered can be an intriguing one; it doesn't necessarily lead to hate." [2] It is also true, however, that Clavell's prison experience heightened his sense of identification with his novel's hero: "It occurred to me that he was a man rather like myself, in an alien land." [3] And, as Henry Smith has pointed out, Blackthorne, the hero of *Shōgun*, is like Clavell in that both first encounter the Japanese as prisoners, in fear of their lives. "If Part I of *Shōgun* (and the first three-hour segment of the TV miniseries) seems disturbingly like a catalog of stereotypes of Japanese violence and barbarity from the Pacific War, one must remember that Clavell has real personal memories of undeniable Japanese inhumanity." [4]

But *Shōgun* is also the story of Blackthorne's growing admiration for Japanese values and ways of doing things. Thus Clavell skillfully leads the western reader—who may be irritated, mystified, or dubious upon first encountering Japanese customs—to a slow appreciation of such things as eating raw fish, sleeping on tatami, or participating in a tea ceremony. Clavell even attempts, though none too accurately, to teach his readers some basic Japanese. And the opening three-hour television segment of *Shōgun* tried to give viewers a genuine taste of Blackthorne's initial confusion in a strange land by having all the Japanese actors speak Japanese and not translating their dialogue.

Shōgun was also designed to teach Americans some Japanese history. The story of John Blackthorne is loosely based on the true story of William Adams, an English pilot whose Dutch ship was wrecked off the coast of Japan in 1600. Adams, whom the

Japanese called "Anjin-sama," or "The Pilot" (just as they do the hero in Clavell's novel), remained in Japan to become an adviser to Tokugawa Ieyasu, the shogun or feudal overlord whom Clavell has renamed Toranaga. As Clavell portrays in his novel, before becoming shogun, Ieyasu faced opposition to his rule from numerous other feudal lords, some of whom were in league with Portuguese traders and Jesuit missionaries. Adams helped create a countervailing force by encouraging Japan's trade with Holland and England, which ultimately led the shogun to restrict the activities of the Portuguese and Spanish and, in 1614, to expel from Japan all the Catholic priests and missionaries. The real William Adams died in Japan of natural causes on May 16, 1620.

Clavell has compressed the action of his novel into a mere six months—from the shipwreck in April 1600 to the eve of the decisive October battle of Sekigahara, in which most of the remaining enemies of the shogun were destroyed. Clavell has also changed the names of all the historical characters and invented a love affair between Blackthorne and the wife of a high-placed feudal lord. (The real William Adams took a Japanese wife and even had two children by her, but she was the daughter of an innkeeper, and hence of the merchant and not the samurai class.)

In his effort to contrast Japanese and western ways, Clavell has made interesting use of the fact that his hero's adventure occurs in 1600—at precisely the time of Shakespeare and Elizabeth's reign in England. (Elizabeth I died in 1603, Shakespeare in 1616.) Thus Englishmen's uncouth eating habits, their lack of regular baths, and (according to Clavell) prudish sexual attitudes are contrasted sharply with the far more sophisticated practices of the Japanese. (Anyone who has read Shakespeare's comedies or the poetry of John Donne and Sir Philip Sidney may doubt that Elizabethan England was as sexually repressed as Clavell makes it out to have been, but the novel is probably accurate in contrasting Japan's relaxed attitudes toward homosexuality with those of Europe.)

Stereotypes in *Shōgun*

Shōgun, like Oliver Statler's *Japanese Inn*, presents a slice of Japanese history and culture in a very palatable form. But whereas Statler plays down the violence of the samurai and stresses instead their interest in Zen and arts such as the Noh drama, Clavell emphasizes their implacability and warlike character. Above all, he presents with full force the Japanese stereotype of cruel men and strong but compliant women. In the words of one of *Shōgun*'s Portuguese characters:

> Of course, all Jappos are different from us—they don't feel pain or cold like us—but samurai are even worse. They fear nothing, least of all death. Why? Only God knows, but it's the truth. If their superiors say "kill," they kill, "die," and they'll fall on their swords or slit their own bellies open. They kill and die as easily as we piss. Women're samurai too, Ingeles. They'll kill to protect their masters, that's what they call their husbands here, or they'll kill themselves if they're told to. They do it by slitting their throats. Here a samurai can order his wife to kill herself and that's what she's got to do, by law. Jesu Madonna, the women are something else though, a different species, Ingeles, nothing on earth like them, but the men. . . . Samurai're reptiles and the safest thing to do is treat them like poisonous snakes.[5]

Clavell reinforces this picture of the fanatical Japanese male by having his characters make certain remarks which, although supposedly spoken in 1600, are clearly intended to remind the reader of future events. A Portuguese friar warns Blackthorne: "Never join Japanese ferocity with modern weapons and modern methods. Or on land they will destroy us."[6] And one Japanese samurai tells another: "With barbarian knowledge, Naga-san, we could take Peking. Whoever takes Peking eventually controls China. And whoever controls China can control the world."[7] Clavell also retails some stereotypes about the differences between Chinese and Japanese: "he [a westerner] thought how much more difficult it was to deal with Japanese than with Chinese. The Chinese understood the art of negotiation, of compromise and concession and reward. But the Japanese were pride-filled and when a man's pride was injured—any Japanese, not just samurai—then death was a small price to repay the insult." [8]

The Japanese woman is presented by Clavell in several guises. There is the quiet, servant-like Fujiko, whom the shogun gives to Blackthorne as a wife:

> "She's recently widowed. She's only nineteen, Anjin-san, poor girl, but she lost a husband and a son and is filled with remorse. To be a formal consort to you would give her a new life."
>
> "What happened to her husband and son?"
>
> Mariko hesitated, distressed at Blackthorne's impolite directness. But she knew enough about him by now to understand that this was *his* custom and not meant as lack of manners. "They were put to death, Anjin-san. While you're here you will need someone to look after your house. The Lady Fujiko will be—"
>
> "Why were they put to death?"
>
> "Her husband almost caused the death of Lord Toranaga. Please con—"
>
> "Toranaga ordered their deaths?"
>
> "Yes. But he was correct. Ask her—she will agree, Anjin-san."
>
> "How old was the child?"
>
> "A few months, Anjin-san."
>
> "Toranaga had an infant put to death for something the father did?"
>
> "Yes. It's our custom. Please be patient with us. In some things we are not free. Our customs are different from yours. You see, by law, we belong to our liege lord. By law a father possesses the lives of his children and wife and consorts and servants. By law his life is possessed by his liege lord. This is our custom."
>
> "So a father can kill anyone in his house?"
>
> "Yes."
>
> "Then you're a nation of murderers." . . .
>
> Mariko took hold of herself. "I beg you to accept her formally. She can help you greatly, teach you if you wish to learn. If you prefer, think of her as nothing—as this wooden post or the shoji screen, or as a rock in your garden—anything you wish, but allow her to stay. If you won't have her as a consort, be merciful. Accept her and then, as head of the house, according to our law, kill her." [9]

Mariko, the heroine of Clavell's novel, is like Michener's Hana-ogi: intelligent, sensual, devoted, but also strong-willed and brave. Like Hana-ogi (and no doubt countless real-life Japanese women) she is the hero's guide to all things Japanese:

"We don't eat foods like you do, so our cooking is more simple. Just rice and a little fish, raw mostly, or cooked over charcoal with a sharp sauce and pickled vegetables, a little soup perhaps. No meat—never meat. We're a frugal people—we have to be, only so little of our land, perhaps a fifth of our soil, can be cultivated—and we're many. With us it's a virtue to be frugal, even in the amount of food we eat."

"Love is a Christian word, Anjin-san. Love is a Christian thought, a Christian ideal. We have no word 'love' as I understand you to mean it. Duty, loyalty, honor, respect, desire, those words and thoughts are what we have, all that we need."

"You see, Anjin-san," she had told him that very special evening when they were finishing the last of many last flasks of sake and he had been joking about the lack of privacy everywhere—people always around and paper walls, ears and eyes always prying, "here you have to learn to create your own privacy. We're taught from childhood to disappear within ourselves, to grow impenetrable walls behind which we live. If we couldn't, we'd all certainly go mad and kill each other and ourselves."

He remembered what Mariko had told him about compartments of the mind: "Be Japanese, Anjin-san, you must, to survive. Do what we do, surrender yourself to the rhythm of *karma* unashamed. Be content with the forces beyond your control. Put all things into their own separate compartments and yield to the *wa*, the harmony of life. Yield, Anjin-san, *karma* is *karma, neh?*" [10]

Clavell also provides a portrait of another type of female some of his male readers may have encountered in real life: the shrewd, money-grasping "Mama-san" of a brothel, here depicted in the character of Gyoko. And he attempts to convey some of the earthiness of old Japanese peasant women, although one doubts that such words were ever spoken in 1600: Toranaga offers one of his former consorts, now elderly, a cup of tea, and she responds: "So sorry, not for me, Great Lord, with your permission, but my back teeth're floating from so much cha and the bucket's a long way away for these old bones." [11]

Despite much talk in *Shōgun* about acceptance of one's karma and other Zen-like practices and attitudes, the overwhelming impression the book conveys is of a violent society in which might makes right. This is perhaps not inaccurate for the historical period being portrayed, but the western reader is likely to transfer such samurai images directly into the present. Such a linking of past and present becomes quite explicit in two novels that followed *Shōgun* onto the best-seller list. *The Ninja* and *The Miko*, by Eric Van Lustbader, were blatant attempts to transplant *Shōgun* into the twentieth century; and it was surely no accident that the paperback covers of all three novels featured a samurai sword partly withdrawn from its scabbard.

Lustbader's *The Ninja* and *The Miko*

The Ninja was published in mid-1980, precisely at the time *Shōgun* was appearing on television, and many people no doubt bought the novel thinking they were getting more of the same. *The Ninja* enjoyed 22 weeks on the best-seller list and was still selling briskly in paperback when, in 1984, its sequel *The Miko* came out. It, too, was a best-seller, but somewhat more briefly.[12]

Lustbader's *The Ninja* is, in essence, *Shōgun* brought up to date. Instead of Japan in 1600, the novel is set in 1980, with flashbacks to World War II and the 1960s. Instead of Black-thorne, an Englishman who comes to understand the ways of Japan, the hero of both *The Ninja* and *The Miko* is Nicholas Linnear, the son of an English colonel and a half-Chinese/half-Japanese mother. Nicholas was born and raised in postwar Japan, but he has nevertheless studied the ancient arts of *bujutsu* (the martial arts) and *ninjutsu* ("the art of stealth"). Nicholas is thus a *ninja* himself, albeit a good *ninja*, who uses his dangerous skills only in self-defense. His chief adversary in the first novel, a Japanese cousin named Saigō, is an evil *ninja* who has mastered some additional tricks such as hypnotizing or temporarily mesmerizing his victims. Evil *ninjas*, according to Lustbader, also tend to psych themselves up with hallucinogens, and for relaxation they indulge in sexual perversions.

Of course Lustbader had read *Shōgun*, and in *The Ninja* he even attempts to show up Clavell by retelling the story on which *Shōgun* was based, with all the proper historical names restored.[13] *The Ninja* also includes two ritual suicides, and *The*

Miko features an earthquake straight out of *Shōgun* rather than real life, in which the earth splits apart in deep fissures that swallow people whole before closing again. There is also much talk about *wa*, used by both Clavell and Lustbader to refer to a state of inner harmony, whereas in Japanese the term is used primarily to refer to social harmony.

The action of *The Ninja* takes place primarily in New York and Long Island, perhaps not surprisingly, since Lustbader has confessed that at the time he wrote the book he had not yet been to Japan.[14] Saigō, the evil *ninja*, has come to New York to kill an American industrialist (at the behest of some Japanese businessmen) as well as Nicholas Linnear, who was once the lover of a Japanese girl also loved by Saigō. The book is punctuated by dozens of lurid killings using traditional *ninja* weapons—poisoned throwing stars, knives, swords, and bare hands. Much of this violence is purely gratuitous, with the victims only peripherally tied into the plot.

The novel also features flashbacks to immediately postwar Japan, and here Lustbader reveals what he has been reading among the scholarly tomes. He is, for example, a follower of the left-wing critics of the occupation who believed that the Japanese *zaibatsu* rather than the military were responsible for starting the war and should therefore have been totally crushed. In a colloquy between the English colonel who is the hero's father and the hero, the colonel says:

"From the first the Americans propounded the myth that the guiding force behind the Japanese war effort came entirely from the military. . . . Nothing could have been further from the truth. It was the members of the *zaibatsu* who backed the country into a corner from which war became the only viable economic alternative."

Nicholas . . . said, "I've read the Constitution, Father. I know that you had a hand in it. It's not Japanese but it's very democratic. Much more so than the policies of the government today. Politically, Japan's gone far to the right, the *zaibatsu* were never dismantled. Most of the prewar personnel is intact. I don't understand that." . . .

"In 1947, Washington, through MacArthur, did a complete about-face.

Rights were withdrawn, certain war-crime convictions were overturned and the leaders of the *zaibatsu* were restored to their prewar eminence." . . .

"Then the Americans deliberately disregarded their own Constitution for Japan, restoring the reactionary *zaibatsu*, guiding us in a right-wing direction."

The Colonel nodded but said nothing.[15]

Clearly Lustbader intends his American readers to absorb the message that the evil wartime *zaibatsu* are still intact and are now waging a new kind of business war on the United States.

By the time he came to write *The Miko* Lustbader had somewhat modified but not basically changed his view of modern Japanese business as war carried on by other means. The reader is treated to a long description of how MITI (the Japanese Ministry of International Trade and Industry), which helped rebuild Japan's postwar economy, had its origins in prewar and wartime ministries. Although not factually inaccurate, the entire sequence of bureaucratic and economic development is made to resemble a devious military plot.[16]

Similarly, Japanese business negotiations are explained in terms of a samurai's code of ethics and strategy. As Nicholas tells his American boss:

"The Japanese knew that you never come to a negotiation showing your true nature. To deal effectively with you, they must find this out. It's called To Move the Shade. It's from the warrior Miyamoto Musashi's guide to strategy. He wrote it in 1645 but all good Japanese businessmen apply his principles to their business practices."

"To Move the Shade," Tomkin said thoughtfully. "What is it?"

"When you cannot see your opponent's true spirit, you make a quick decisive feint attack. As Musashi writes, he will then show his long sword—today we can transform that into meaning his negotiation spirit—thinking he has seen your spirit. But you have shown him nothing of value and he has instead revealed his inner strategy to you."[17]

Unfortunately, Nicholas's expertise on Japanese matters evidently does not extend to informing his boss that Japanese last names usually come first; it is Lord Miyamoto who wrote *The Book of Five Rings*. This book, incidentally, did enjoy a brief real-life vogue in the early 1980s at American business schools, where it was thought to contain important Japanese business precepts. The search for Japanese secrets of the marketplace was not dissimilar to the vogue, in the late 1950s, for the Japanese secrets of inner harmony, presumably to be found in Zen *kōans* such as the sound of one hand clapping.

Like *Shōgun*, Lustbader's two novels are full of cultural tidbits—some accurate, some not. *The Miko*, for example, will teach the reader something about the drinking habits of Japanese men, a Japanese wedding ceremony, and the etiquette of the Japanese bath. On the other hand, *The Miko* features a Japanese executive who has as his bodyguard an ex–sumo champion still wearing the traditional topknot—an impossibility in real life, because a sumo wrestler's hair is cut off in a special ceremony when he retires from the ring.[18] And it is highly misleading for Lustbader to refer to Japan's contemporary police force as the Kempeitai; the Kempeitai were the much-feared and hated military police of prewar and wartime Japan, and were disbanded in 1945.[19]

Like Clavell, Lustbader is also interested in characterizing the differences between the Chinese and the Japanese. In *The Miko*, the Chinese are depicted as devious, corrupt, and clever, but also as sensual and not nearly as disciplined as the Japanese: "For more than three hours they feasted and in true Chinese fashion talked of nothing of serious import during that time. The Chinese—as opposed to the Japanese, who were far more fanatic about business—believed that nothing should take away from the savoring of a meal. In that respect they were the French of the Far East."[20] At the same time, Lustbader believes that the Japanese will gravitate toward the Communist Chinese because both are Asian nations:

"Would you rather have the Russians link arms with China? What kind of position do you think that would put Japan in? I don't think even America's might could save us then." He spread his hands. "Don't you see, Nangi-san? By providing this [Chinese] faction with a unique kind of ammunition, you will gain an incredibly direct foothold into Peking, the Forbidden City. Lo Whan's faction will owe us much. And in time they will have to repay that debt. The price will be up to us to negotiate."

"But they are *Chinese*," Nangi protested. "They are Communists."

"They're also Asian."[21]

Lustbader's portrayal of Japanese women conforms to the Madame Butterfly stereotype of being both gentle and strong: "She looked like a tiny doll, Nicholas thought, a perfect porcelain thing to be put on a pedestal inside a glass case, protected from the elements. In fact, Itami needed no such exterior protection; she had a will of iron and the power to promote it, even with her husband, Satsugai."[22] Some of the younger women, however, particularly the two with whom the hero falls in love, are not only traditionally beautiful and sensual but also violent. Thus Lustbader, perhaps in a bow toward sexual equality, has grafted the Japanese male stereotype of the cold-blooded samurai onto the more pliable female stereotype. Nonetheless, the first heroine, whom the hero suspects of having betrayed him, proves to be utterly loyal to the point of sacrificing her life for him. The second girl, Akiko, has trained herself to be a female *ninja* and has become a sorceress, a *miko*. Although she has one passionate scene with the hero, she's basically out to kill him. In the course of the novel *The Miko*, she stabs at least three men to death with her dagger and cuts up several more with her samurai sword and a steel-edged fan. No wonder the hero is ultimately glad to get back to his American girlfriend. The dangers of loving a Japanese woman were never more vividly displayed.

Above all, what a reader imbibes from Lustbader's novels is a renewed impression that the sword-wielding samurai of the 1600s, the fierce and determined Japanese soldiers of the 1940s, and the aggressive, hard-working businessmen of the 1980s are all one and the same. As Nicholas's revered *bujutsu* teacher tells him shortly after the end of the war:

"No matter what happens to Japan, *bushido* [the Way of the Warrior] will never completely perish. We begin to wear Western business suits, our women wear their hair in the American manner; we adopt Western ways. These things do not matter. The Japanese is like the willow, bending in the wind so that it should not break. These are merely outward manifestations of our desire now for parity in the world. So, too, do the Americans unwittingly serve our purpose, for, with their money, we shall rise more powerful than ever. Yet we must ever look to our tradition, for only *bushido* makes us strong."[23]

In the mid-1960s, the advertising executive Jerry Della Femina suggested facetiously that a campaign for some then-new electronic imports by Panasonic might feature ads telling the American consumer they came "from those wonderful folks who gave you Pearl Harbor."[24] At the time, this was regarded as a typical piece of black humor. But as the previously discussed article by Theodore White in the *New York Times Magazine* of July 1985 made clear, twenty years later Japanese prowess was no longer a joking matter. Some Americans, particularly members of unions that had lost jobs because of Japanese imports, regarded Japan as every bit as much of an enemy as it had been during World War II. It is sobering to recall that on July 19, 1982, a Detroit automobile worker and his stepson beat a Chinese man to death with a baseball bat *because they thought he was Japanese.* Perhaps even more ominous, the two men, though convicted of manslaughter, were sentenced to only three years on probation.

Thus, in many ways, American attitudes toward Japan had come full circle in the forty years since 1945. As Lee Iacocca, the chief executive officer of Chrysler and former President of the Ford Motor Company, put it in his 1985 best-selling autobiography: "Right now, we're in the midst of another major war with Japan. This time it's not a shooting war, and I guess we should be thankful for that. The current conflict is a trade war. But because our government refuses to see this war for what it really is, we're well on the road to defeat."[25] The history behind this attitude is the subject of the next chapter.

EIGHT

The Business Nexus

ALL THE AMERICAN stereotypes with regard to
Japan have undergone changes over the years, but in no area
have the shifts been more dramatic than in the field of business.
During and immediately after the war, some Americans called
for the complete destruction of Japan's industries and of her
"war-making potential." Yet by 1947, the occupation was already launched on its "reverse course," designed to rebuild
Japan's economy. In 1949, the *Saturday Evening Post* published
an article entitled "We're Giving Japan Democracy, but She
Can't Earn Her Living," in which the occupation was criticized
for not doing more to build up Japan. In May 1951, shortly before the end of the occupation, *Fortune* asked, "Can Japan Pay
Her Own Way?" and answered the question in only a guardedly
optimistic fashion; and in 1954, in an article entitled "Japan:
Help Needed," *Fortune* was still worrying about Japan's dwin-
dling foreign exchange because her imports were far exceeding
exports. Yet two years later U.S. textile manufacturers were already calling for import quotas on Japanese-made textiles, and
by 1957 *Fortune* was trumpeting that "defeated in war, stripped
of colonies, never rich in resources, Japan has reemerged as the
foremost industrial power in Asia."[1]

As American attitudes toward Japan's economic viability changed, so also did the attitudes toward Japanese products themselves. In the immediate postwar period, just as before the war, Americans regarded Japanese-made items as cheap and shoddily made. In 1949, *Business Week* reported that "war and occupation have not changed Japan's traditional tendency to dump poor-quality products on world markets. American engineers here are convinced of this after rejecting thousands of dollars worth of Japanese manufactures that didn't even come close to contract specifications."[2] The article goes on to give details about a $300,000 shipment of transformers of which only 1 percent were usable, and a $700,000 shipment of radio equipment for Korea of which only one-seventh of the units worked. When an official of the Wireless Communication Equipment Industrial Association of Japan tried to answer some of these charges, *Business Week* in effect ridiculed Japanese business still further by printing the letter without editorial changes. Written in somewhat quaint English, the letter tried to explain that not all the defects could be blamed on the manufacturers because

a part of the shipments were carried by trucks all the criggy way to Seoul, where the goods were hurled down in such a senseless way, thus subsequently caused considerable damages after all. While the rest of the shipment were left untouched outside the godowns over six months, on some of which naturally caused electrical inefficiencies, and there found those still practically workable is nothing but two-thirds of all.[3]

Nonetheless, only two years later, in mid-1951, Japanese manufacturers held a successful 18-day trade fair in Seattle, where they displayed 8,000 items ranging from knickknacks to cultured pearls, bicycles, canned fish, and sewing machines. *Business Week* reported that "at first buyers were dubious about the quality of Japan's products. But now, with the fair over, the consensus is that there's been real improvement over prewar. Some items—like cameras, binoculars, sewing machines—were felt to be right up to U.S. standards."[4] In 1957, *Business Week* accorded Nikon and Canon an even higher accolade when it ranked their products "in the same category as German cam-

"Japanese manufacturers competent for making atomic bomb more cheaper, saving American gentleman many dollars. Yes please?"

eras."[5] It also pointed out that Japanese manufacturers were beginning to appeal to the "quality market" in a number of other fields, and it quoted one American importer who predicted "a whole new group of Japanese products, based on Japan's great artistic traditions, can change U.S. homes as much as the Scandinavian-modern designs did in the 1930s and the 1940s."[6] This is, of course, precisely what happened, except that the products that changed American lives were less in the realm of fine arts than in high-tech: color television sets, hi-fi components, videotape recorders, and—of course—automobiles.

In a general way, it is clear that the postwar American image of the Japanese economy changed, in accordance with actual changes in Japan, from one of great weakness to one of great strength. One way to illustrate this is with several cartoons. The first, from the September 30, 1945, *New York Times Magazine*

But aren't you afraid if we buy a Japanese car we'll be letting down the whales?

*"Your race horses, your wines, your philanthropy to Ivy
League colleges, your works of art—really, Teddy,
you're practically Japanese."*

Drawing by William Hamilton; © 1973 the New Yorker Magazine, Inc.

(see p. 125), pokes fun at the Japanese willingness to copy any
foreign product and produce it more cheaply than the original. The second (see p. 126), dating from 1974, pokes fun not at
the Japanese but at Americans trying to balance their consumer
interest in a Japanese car against their ecological concern for
whales, which were then (and still are) being overhunted by the
Japanese whaling industry. The third (see above), also from the

Oh, come on. A dinner for two will have no appreciable effect on their huge national trade surplus.

Reprinted by permission: Tribune Media Services.

mid-1970s, comments on the strength of the Japanese economy by depicting its investors, rather than Americans, as international pacesetters.* The last two cartoons (see above and p. 129),

*This cartoon had an interesting real-life counterpart more than a decade later, when on April 8, 1987, the Yasuda Fire and Marine Insurance Company of Tokyo paid $39.85 million for one of Vincent van Gogh's paintings of sunflowers—the highest price ever paid for a single painting at an art auction. What most U.S. commentators failed to note, however, was that another Japanese businessman, Koyata

"These Tokyo nights can be chilly . . . throw some more dollars on the fire."

© San Francisco Chronicle 1978. Reprinted by permission.

both from 1978, reveal the increasing concern of the United States over its trade imbalance with Japan.

As we have noted, at the same time that Americans were changing their impressions of the Japanese economy, their impressions of Japanese products were changing. They stopped thinking of them as cheap, shoddy, and gimcrack, and began to

---

Yamamoto, had owned one of van Gogh's sunflower paintings before the war but that it was destroyed during a World War II American bombing raid. So perhaps Yasuda's purchase is less a case of parvenu spending than of "Living well is the best revenge." See Sam Jameson, "What's Behind that $39-Million Bouquet?" *Los Angeles Times*, April 10, 1987, part 6, p. 1.

regard them as highly reliable, precision-made, and well designed. By the 1970s, many Americans were deliberately buying Japanese-made radios, television sets, and automobiles because they believed them to be *better* than comparable American-made items, and many more Americans were buying Japanese-made products without knowing their country of origin because they were sold under American brand names. When President Ford visited Japan in November 1974, he presented a group of Japanese Diet members with portable cassette recorders, which turned out, underneath their American trade mark, to be discreetly marked "Made in Japan."[7]

By the mid-1980s, when American trade deficits with Japan were running between thirty and fifty billion dollars, public perceptions about Japanese products changed yet again. According to a nation-wide poll conducted by the *Los Angeles Times*, September 20–26, 1985, 60 percent of those questioned said they preferred products made in the United States and 44 percent said they always checked whether something was made in the United States or abroad. Nonetheless, 29 percent thought that Japan made the best television sets (and this figure rose to 52 percent of those with college educations), and 42 percent thought Japan made the best cameras. Moreover, 57 percent had knowingly bought something made in Japan during the preceding three years—24 percent some piece of electronic equipment, and 12 percent a Japanese car. (In this poll, 18 percent of those questioned owned one or more Japanese cars.)[8]

I use the word "knowingly," because by 1985 it had become still more problematic to identify whether a product was made in Japan or the United States. Sony and Honda, to name only two manufacturers that most Americans recognized as being Japanese, had opened factories in the United States, staffed with American workers. Several models of cars sold by General Motors and Chrysler were actually made in Japan, but Toyota and General Motors had also opened a joint-venture plant in Fremont, California, that was producing a small Chevrolet. On the other hand, no videotape recorders, regardless of whether they were marketed under a Japanese label or an American brand name such as RCA or Fisher, were made in the United States.

From Aid, to Trade, to Protectionism?

A somewhat more detailed look at American attitudes toward Japanese business reveals that they have fluctuated over the years more or less in accordance with the nature, quality, and size of that business. Up until the end of the occupation, there was considerable doubt about the quality of Japanese goods, although this rapidly disappeared when the newly independent Japanese government began to allow exporters to set up trade associations and began a rigid program of quality controls for exports. In 1953, *Business Week* wrote an article full of admiration for "Japan's effort to rebuild its U.S. markets . . . a dogged, unobtrusive business operation—more businesslike than it ever was before the war."[9] In 1954, the magazine reported that "The U.S. has decided to go all out to bring Japan into the General Agreement on Tariffs and Trade (GATT), the free world trading community, as a full member." It acknowledged that Europe and the Commonwealth were fearful of Japanese competition, and that some U.S. industries were also highly vulnerable, but it argued that under GATT Japan's entry into foreign markets would be spread across the free world. At that time there was a good deal of concern about keeping the Japanese economy healthy so that it would not be forced into the orbit of Communist China. Already in 1953, *Business Week* reported that Sumitomo Chemical was operating at only 60 percent of capacity and was "straining at the bit for more sales."[10]

It was not until 1955 that Japanese–U.S. trade began to surpass prewar levels. American stores in that year were carrying primarily Japanese-made toys, cameras, chinaware, sewing machines, furniture, ladies' blouses, cashmere sweaters, silks, Christmas ornaments, and pearls, although Japan was also exporting plywood, tuna, and cotton cloth to the United States (this last made from imported American raw cotton). As a result of the GATT agreements, the United States had made tariff concessions on imports of cotton cloth, chinaware, toys, and Christmas decorations; but California fishing interests demanded a duty on Japanese tuna, and there was also a great deal of pressure for tariffs on such things as "the notorious dollar blouse." Japanese market researchers, it seems, had determined that there would be a large demand for a simple cotton blouse that could be sold across the United States for $1, and to the consternation of American manufacturers, more than a million orders were in fact placed. *Business Week* and other economic writers were sympathetic to Japan and pointed out that it was the largest single market for American raw cotton: in 1955, Japan bought some 647,000 bales, 25 percent of the total the United States exported.[11] Nonetheless, in early January 1957, Japan yielded to the pressures of U.S. textile manufacturers and placed a voluntary quota on its shipments of cotton textiles to the United States.

During the first week of November 1961, a cabinet-level U.S.–Japan Committee on Trade and Economic Affairs met at Hakone, but there was not much agreement between the two countries about their growing trade gap. (Japan was then *importing* $1 billion worth of goods more than it was exporting to the United States.) Japan wanted restrictions on Japanese exports to the United States relaxed, whereas the United States wanted the Japanese "to broaden the base of their international trade with other countries of Asia and with Europe," despite the fact that a number of European countries had (and have) even stiffer barriers against Japanese products than the United States does. In effect the Japanese succeeded in achieving both these goals during the 1960s, so that by 1970 it was exporting $19 billion worth of goods worldwide, almost $6 billion of it to the United States, which by then had a trade deficit with Japan.

The 1960s was a period of tremendous economic growth for Japan—growth so rapid that many of us tend to forget how recent some of Japan's industrial strength is. For example, Honda and Yamaha only began to sell motorcycles in the United States in 1960; yet by 1966, Honda, Yamaha, and Suzuki between them sold approximately 400,000 motorcycles in the United States, 85 percent of all U.S. sales.[12] Japan did not begin producing passenger automobiles until the late 1950s, and then its production went exclusively for taxis and rental car companies in Japan. Not until 1964 did Toyota ship fifty Coronas to the United States to test consumer reactions. In 1974, it sold American consumers 238,135 cars, and by 1984 this figure had more than doubled to 482,790. Overall Japanese car exports to the U.S. totaled 1.85 million by 1984, and this figure was artificially low because of a "voluntary" Japanese quota.

At the same time that the high quality of Japanese products was winning American customers, the United States's growing trade deficit with Japan (see Table 3) once again began to produce a clamor among American manufacturers for tariff barriers and quotas. Between 1969 and 1971 there was another prolonged effort by the U.S. textile industry to limit imports of Japanese woolen and man-made fibers. The dispute was finally settled by an "orderly marketing agreement" instead of an imposition of tariffs by the United States.[13] In 1971, the United States also forced an upward revaluation of the yen, hoping that this would help correct its trade imbalance with Japan. The Japanese were fearful that the sudden increase in the cost of their exports would lead to a dramatic drop in sales, but this proved not to be the case. Japanese exports to the United States continued to climb, and the U.S. trade deficit with Japan continued to grow. In mid-1977, the United States tried to limit the imports of Japanese television sets. By 1981, the American automobile industry had successfully lobbied for "voluntary" quotas on the numbers of Japanese cars to be sent to the United States each year. When in early 1985 President Reagan said that he would allow the four-year agreement to lapse, the Japanese promptly announced that they would send the United States an additional 450,000 cars

TABLE 3

Japanese-U.S. Trade

($ millions)

Year	Japanese imports from U.S.	Japanese exports to U.S.	Year	Japanese imports from U.S.	Japanese exports to U.S.
1952	768.3	234.3	1970	5,559.6	5,939.8
1953	759.7	233.9	1971	4,977.9	7,495.3
1954	848.7	282.6	1972	5,851.6	8,847.7
1955	773.9	456.2	1973	9,269.6	9,448.7
1956	1,067.2	550.4	1974	12,700.0	12,800.0
1957	1,623.1	604.5	1975	11,608.1	11,148.6
1958	1,956.1	690.7	1976	11,809.3	15,689.6
1959	1,115.6	1,046.6	1977	12,396.1	19,716.9
1960	1,553.5	1,101.6	1978	14,790.4	24,914.7
1961	2,095.8	1,066.9	1979	20,430.8	26,402.5
1962	1,809.0	1,400.2	1980	24,408.0	31,367.3
1963	2,077.3	1,506.9	1981	25,297.1	38,608.8
1964	2,336.0	1,841.6	1982	24,179.2	36,329.9
1965	2,366.1	2,479.2	1983	24,647.5	42,828.8
1966	2,657.7	2,969.5	1984	26,862.0	59,937.3
1967	3,212.1	3,012.0	1985	25,296.5	68,637.8
1968	3,527.4	4,086.5	1986	29,054.0	80,456.0
1969	4,089.9	4,957.8	1987	31,442.0	83,580.0

SOURCE: Japanese government, Ministry of International Trade and Industry.

during the coming year—a 25 percent increase. Interestingly enough, it was not only the American automobile industry that was upset by these developments: the *Los Angeles Times* poll of September 1985 revealed that 58 percent of those questioned opposed Reagan's action and only 34 percent favored it. Democrats were somewhat more strongly opposed (67 percent to 28 percent) than Republicans (53 percent to 41 percent). Only college graduates registered 50 percent in favor of Reagan's lifting of auto quotas, with 43 percent of them opposed.

How did Americans formulate such views? During the late 1970s and early 1980s, newspapers and magazines were full of stories about the Japanese–U.S. trade imbalance. Some of these stories blamed the Japanese for maintaining unfair trade barriers against such American products as telecommunications equipment, pharmaceuticals, farm products, lumber, tobacco, and beef. Others charged that the Japanese engaged in "dumping" goods in foreign markets (charging lower prices abroad than they did at home), and that Japanese wages were much lower than comparable American wages, giving their products an unfair advantage. (Actually, by the 1980s American and Japanese wages and standards of living were roughly comparable.) More even-handed analysts pointed out that Japanese factories, having been built largely after the war, were more modern than American factories, and that they were increasingly automated, leading to lower unit costs and fewer product defects. By the mid-1980s the U.S. dollar was also exceedingly strong compared to other currencies, particularly the yen. This not only made American goods more expensive overseas, but it made Japanese imports relatively cheap for Americans to buy.

It is not clear, however, how much of this information was absorbed by readers. The September 1985 *Los Angeles Times* poll revealed much confusion. For example, 49 percent of those asked "Do you think buying goods from other countries and selling goods to other countries—in other words, foreign trade—does it help this nation's economy, or hurt this nation's economy?" answered that they thought foreign trade hurt the nation's economy. Sixty-four percent also thought that it was a good thing for the country that the U.S. dollar had risen sharply in value against foreign currencies. And while 62 percent said they favored either quotas or trade barriers for Japanese products, 57 percent recognized that such restrictions would raise consumer prices, and 46 percent thought that raising trade barriers would cause the United States to suffer in the long run.

It may be that such responses reflect a residual isolationist and "fortress America" attitude that has long been strong in the United States, and that has occasionally guided national policy, as it did during the 1920s and 1930s. Or it may be that the problems of international trade and balances of payments are simply too complex to be understood by a majority of the general public. Whatever the case, by the mid-1980s a sizable gap had developed in the United States between opinion leaders and the average voter on the issue of Japan. Many influential figures in government, the universities, and the media argued that barriers against imports would inevitably provoke retaliation that would further damage American industries and farms, as well as causing a sharp increase in the domestic cost of living. But those who held elected positions were often under fierce pressure from business and labor union lobbyists and their constituents to promote protectionist legislation. What the outcome of this tug of war will be remains uncertain.

Learning from Japan

One constructive trend that emerged during the late 1970s as the United States felt increasingly challenged by Japan's powerful economy was a move to learn how Japan did it. Just as many American consumers openly admired the quality of Japanese goods, so American business leaders became curious why Japanese factories worked so well and turned out products with so few defects. A book that helped start this process of self-reflection was Ezra Vogel's *Japan as Number 1: Lessons for America*. Published in 1979 by Harvard University Press, this book was not on the best-seller list in the United States, although by 1983 it had gone through eight paperback printings.[14] It was widely discussed in magazines and read on college campuses, particularly in business schools.

Professor Vogel described various aspects of Japanese society: the high-quality (and high-pressure) education system; cooperation between government and business; the organization of large companies; and the systems of welfare and crime control. In all these areas, he argued, Japan does things better than the United States and we need to learn from and adapt her techniques. He acknowledged that this might be difficult because there are some basic differences between the two societies: Americans tend to value individualism whereas Japanese are more group-oriented; the United States has a much more heterogeneous population and many more immigrant groups than racially and socially ho-

"I love you more than anything else in the world—excluding my job at Yamada Electric, of course."

mogeneous Japan; and the governments of the two nations, while superficially similar in that both are constitutional democracies, actually function quite differently. Nonetheless, Vogel called for a reorientation and rejuvenation of many aspects of American society.

"Today we'll be talking about some new approaches."

Such major shifts can and do occur in societies without prior recourse to war or revolution, but they are rare. Japan during the occupation, and the United States after the Civil War and again after the depression initiated vast, deliberate social changes. But it seemed unlikely that Americans in the mid-1980s as yet felt sufficiently threatened to undertake anything on this scale. Many smaller groups in the society, however, particularly in the

"This is Teddy Bonesteel. Teddy is rapidly becoming competitive with Japan."

Drawing by Weber; © 1987 the New Yorker Magazine, Inc.

U.S. business community, took to heart Vogel's strictures to learn from Japan. This can be illustrated by three amusing cartoons from the mid-1980s. One pokes fun at the large number of articles then being published about how hard Japanese employees worked and how loyal they were to their companies (see p. 137). The second (on p. 138), originally published in the *Wall Street Journal*, is addressed to the sudden craze that developed in American companies for employing Japanese management techniques. The third (above) comments wryly on American businessmen being reduced to playing "catch-up."

Another sign that American business, if not the society as a whole, was taking the Japanese challenge seriously was the appearance of a new and rather unusual best-seller, *Theory Z* by William Ouchi. Written by a Japanese-American professor of business administration and published by a textbook publisher, this book astonished even its author by staying on the best-seller list for 22 weeks during 1981 and selling more than 150,000 copies in hardcover.

Whereas Vogel's book was sweeping and, in many ways, impractical in its suggestions, William Ouchi's book, despite its enigmatic title, was practical and aimed directly at business managers. Like Vogel, Ouchi pinpointed certain ways in which American companies differed from Japanese companies. For example:

In the United States we conduct our careers between organizations but within a single specialty. In Japan people conduct careers between specialties but within a single organization. This is a fundamental difference in the way that our two nations have dealt with the problem of industrialization. In the United States companies specialize their jobs and individuals specialize their careers. As a result a semiconductor specialist, a portfolio manager, or a personnel manager can be moved from company A to company B and within five days all can be working effectively. . . . In Japan it is difficult to take a worker from one company, move that person to another company, and expect him ever to be fully productive. Japanese do not specialize only in a technical field; they also specialize in an organization, in learning how to make a specific, unique business operate as well as it possibly can.[15]

Ouchi argues that the sort of loyalty elicited by Japanese companies (he calls them J-type companies) can be found in a few very unusual and quite successful American companies. He studied these special American (Z-type) companies, and their management techniques proved to be similar to those of J-type companies and quite different from those of the run-of-the-mill American (A-type) company. The bulk of his book is a primer for managers who wish to change their A-type company into a Z-type one.

In many ways, Ouchi's book is quintessentially American. Although he has a Japanese last name and cites Japanese organizational techniques to bolster his arguments, his is a more intelligent version of *The One-Minute Manager* or *How to Win Friends and Influence People*. Ouchi is even convinced that if more American companies became Z-type companies, in which people worked "in an integrated and supportive working environment," the national divorce rate would go down because people would feel less stress.[16] As far as Japanese business is concerned, he finds much to admire. But his chief message to American business is that

Successful Z companies and others like them have forged a response to the Japanese challenge. They have understood that the real challenge from Japan is not to undercut their prices, not to re-automate our plants, nor to erect trade barriers. Neither is it to see whether we can mimic the art of Japanese management. The challenge is to understand and to acknowledge a distinctively American approach to management, to realize that it has stayed the same for two hundred years, and to apply our ingenuity to the development of new organizational and managerial solutions.[17]

A similar message, in an even more accessible form, was put forth in the fall of 1985 by the comic film *Gung Ho*. This American-made film deals with the efforts of a Pennsylvania town to persuade a Japanese auto manufacturer to reopen its closed auto plant (put out of business by Japanese competition). The movie is full of crude stereotypes of both Japanese and Americans, used for comic effect. The Japanese bosses are portrayed as work-obsessed martinets, wholly preoccupied with the quality and quantity of the cars produced. A boss whose wife is about to have a baby does not leave his post to be by her side. By contrast, an American worker demands time off when his son is having his tonsils removed. The American workers are depicted as being skilled and capable of hard work but also as anarchic: they dress sloppily, bring noisy cassette players to work, and brawl and drink after hours. In the end, however, a kind of reconciliation is reached between the American workers and their Japanese bosses. The American shop steward reminds his men about America's traditional "do-or-die spirit" and then comments, "They're [the Japanese] kicking our butts and that ain't luck. . . . They have it and we'd better get it back fast." Meanwhile one of the Japanese managers tells *his* superior, "We work too damned hard. . . . Our friends, our families should be our lives. . . . We have things we can learn from Americans."

William Ouchi and *Gung Ho* reflected the thinking of many Americans in the mid-1980s, who concluded that facing up to the challenge of Japanese business might be the best thing that had ever happened to the American economy. If, that is, it woke the United States up in time. If not, then one would predict in the years ahead many more moans and cries of "foul play" and many more demands for quotas and trade barriers against Japan.

Much the same point was made by David Halberstam in his 1986 best-seller *The Reckoning*, which contrasts the troubles of the Ford Motor Company in adjusting to the challenges of the oil shocks with the successes of Nissan Motors. Nor was Halberstam very optimistic in his conclusions:

In some ways, as America faced the future and prepared to find its place in the new and uncertain international economy, it was, contrasted to other leading Western industrial nations, still remarkably blessed. It was rich in land, and its agriculture was productive, modern, and bountiful. It had more mineral resources than any potential industrial competitor. Its venture capital system was probably the most vital in the world. . . . There were two real weaknesses, however. One was the public school system and the low level of literacy. . . . The other respect in which America was ill prepared for the new world economy was in terms of expectations. . . . Few were discussing how best to adjust the nation to an age of somewhat diminished expectations, or how to marshal its abundant resources for survival in a harsh, unforgiving new world.[18]

There is no question that the American image of Japan as a high-technology, powerful, industrialized society is here to stay for the foreseeable future. This image developed only recently, in the mid-1970s, and like many stereotypes it can have either a positive or a negative valence. Viewed positively, Japan's economic strength strikes the American consumer as a great boon, bringing him state-of-the-art television sets and stereo equipment; well-engineered, fuel-efficient automobiles; even high-style fashions and cosmetics. Viewed negatively, Japan's powerful economy and its exports loom as a threat to U.S. jobs and domestic prosperity. As this is being written, the positive and negative valences are still roughly in balance, producing a rather schizophrenic response by Americans to Japanese business. The danger, of course, is that as the trade deficit continues to grow, American attitudes will tip further toward the negative end of the scale.

NINE

The Dilemma of Japanese-Americans

IN 1943, Lieutenant General John L. DeWitt, commander of the U.S. Western Defense Command, argued before a congressional committee that whereas Germans and Italians could be treated as individuals, "a Jap's a Jap. . . . You can't change him by giving him a piece of paper"—that is, by making him a naturalized U.S. citizen.[1] This sort of justification was commonly used to explain why, in the summer of 1942, some 110,000 Japanese-Americans living on the west coast of the United States were herded into concentration camps for the next two-and-a-half years. At the same time, the 160,000 Japanese living in Hawaii, who made up just under 40 percent of the territory's population, remained at liberty. Was there some recognizable difference between these two groups, or did the difference lie in the attitudes of the rest of the population and government authorities? Have popular attitudes toward Japanese-Americans changed since World War II, and is there any connection between such attitudes and American attitudes toward Japan itself?

To some extent, any ethnic group in a large, pluralistic society such as the United States, is a hostage to international relations. Depending on how long ago they left their country of origin and their reasons for leaving, immigrant groups—particularly members of the first generation—are expected to retain strong emotional ties to their native land. For example, Americans are not surprised that many Cubans, even those born in the United States, say they would return to Cuba if the government there were altered. Nor, given the reasons why most Cubans left, do Americans really fear the existence of a large pro-Castro fifth column, even though among the so-called "Mariel boat people"—the people Castro released from prison and allowed to leave in 1980—there are undoubtedly some spies and Castro supporters.

On the other hand, it is not uncommon for violence to be directed against American ethnic groups as a result of international affairs. In 1979–81, at the time of the U.S. embassy hostage crisis in Iran, there was sporadic and localized harassment of Iranians living in the United States, even though most of these Iranians were themselves opposed to and refugees from the Khomeini regime.

The United States also has a long history of ethnic tensions in neighborhoods, schools, and places of business: for example, Polish, Italian, and Irish neighborhoods have fought to keep out blacks; all-white schools have at various times tried to close their doors to Asian, black, and Spanish-speaking children; and unions as well as whole industries have discriminated against various ethnic groups. In many ways it was these sorts of tensions that gave rise to the incarceration of Japanese-Americans during World War II.

Hostility toward "Orientals" in California dates from the 1850s gold rush, when the Forty-Niners tried to limit Chinese fortune-seekers to the poorest, played-out mines, and even then often robbed, beat, or murdered them. In 1857 the Shasta *Republican* declared that "hundreds of Chinamen have been slaughtered in cold blood during the last five years by desperadoes that infest our state. The murder of Chinamen was of almost daily occurrence yet . . . we have heard of but two or three instances where the guilty parties have been brought to justice."[2] As a result, many Chinese moved to the cities, where they opened laundries, restaurants, and small shops and groceries, while others labored on the transcontinental railroad.

With the completion of the railroad in 1869, anti-Chinese sentiment surged among white workers who feared that the Chinese would supplant them in jobs or be used as strike-breakers. In 1877, an Irish immigrant to California, Dennis Kearney, founded the Workingmen's Party, which began to lobby for the total exclusion of all Chinese. This was achieved in 1882, by the so-called Chinese Exclusion Act, banning Chinese immigration for ten years (it was extended in 1892 and again in 1902), and prohibiting the naturalization of those already in the U.S. At the time the original exclusion act was passed, there were approximately 100,000 Chinese in the United States, and only 2,000 Japanese residents; and while the former were mostly peasants from South China, the latter were primarily students and merchants.

The 1880s were difficult years in Japan, particularly in the southern part of Kyushu, where dissident samurai had staged a futile rebellion (the Satsuma Rebellion of 1877) against the newly created Meiji government. The central government found it convenient to ease land hunger and political dissent by encouraging emigration. At the same time, Hawaii, which was still an independent kingdom,[3] was suffering from a labor shortage. In 1875, the United States had ended its tariff on Hawaiian sugar, and white planters began to expand their cane fields and search for new supplies of plantation workers. Initially, much of this labor was brought in under contract: workers' passage to Hawaii was provided in exchange for a guaranteed three years' paid labor. The normal contract specified 26 days of labor each month, with a ten-hour day in the fields or a twelve-hour day in the sugar mills.[4] Between 1886 and 1895, nearly 30,000 Japanese came to Hawaii under contract, all but 5,000 of them men.

Meanwhile, the Hawaiian monarchy was overthrown in 1893, and for a few years Hawaii was a republic, until the rich land-owners engineered its annexation by the United States in 1898. The planters knew, however, that both the Chinese Exclusion

Act and the United States ban on contract labor would henceforth apply to them. So in 1899, after annexation but before congressional legislation had created the territory of Hawaii, another 26,000 Japanese contract laborers were brought in—the largest number ever admitted in a single year.[5] The planters had expected that these new laborers would work the required three years, but in fact under the new territorial law their contracts were immediately declared invalid and the laborers were free. Some returned to Japan, but many left for the mainland of the United States to look for less arduous, better-paying work.

The U.S. census for 1890 counted only 2,039 Japanese in the total population, but by 1900 this figure had grown to 85,437 (24,326 on the mainland and 61,111 in Hawaii).[6] Only a very small percentage, 5.7 percent, were *nisei*, that is, "second generation," born in either Hawaii or the United States. Because of the Chinese Exclusion Act, Japanese workers were needed on the farms and ranches of central California, the lumber camps of Oregon and Washington, and the fishing industry up and down the west coast. Many Japanese began by working as tenant farmers, but some managed to lease land and went into business for themselves, raising strawberries, vegetables, flowers, and fruit trees. Once again, California business groups began to agitate against the "Oriental menace" and tried to have the Japanese included in the 1902 extension of the Chinese Exclusion Act. They failed in this; but in 1906, after the San Francisco earthquake and fire had destroyed a number of schools, the San Francisco school board decreed that henceforth Japanese and Korean children would have to attend the segregated "Chinese" school.

Japan vigorously protested this treatment of its citizens; and because it was now a major world power, having recently defeated Russia in the Russo-Japanese War, President Theodore Roosevelt tried to get the school board to rescind its segregation order. After several months of political pressure and negotiations, the school board was forced to compromise; but Roosevelt in turn obtained from the Japanese what became known as the Gentlemen's Agreement, under which the Japanese virtually stopped all emigration of laborers to the United States. Between 1908 and 1924, the year when Japanese immigration was banned entirely, most of the new Japanese immigrants were "picture brides," who helped equalize the lopsided sex-ratio of the early immigrants and produced the growing generation of *nisei*.

Anti-Japanese sentiment was not lessened by the Gentlemen's Agreement—instead they were now accused of "breeding like rabbits"—and the 1924 Immigration Act was passed, banning Asian immigration altogether. Around the same time California and other west coast states were passing their own stringent laws against landownership by "aliens ineligible for citizenship." The Naturalization Act of 1790 had extended the privilege of becoming naturalized citizens only to "free white persons," and in 1922, in a case brought by Takao Ozawa, the U.S. Supreme Court ruled that since Orientals were not white, they could not be naturalized. Under U.S. law, however, children of foreign nationals born on U.S. soil are automatically citizens. Thus, during the 1930s some Japanese *issei* (first generation, hence ineligible to become citizens) bought land in the name of their *nisei* children. This was, of course, considered a subterfuge by many white landowners and no doubt contributed to the impunity with which Japanese-owned property was confiscated during their World War II imprisonment.

World War II Attitudes

The history of anti-Oriental sentiment and exclusion that I have briefly described here conditioned popular attitudes during World War II. Nonetheless, it would be a mistake to think of the Japanese-Americans purely as victims. As John Stephan amply illustrates in his fascinating book, *Hawaii Under the Rising Sun*, many first-generation Japanese immigrants were proud of Japan's conquests in China and identified with their homeland's military prowess. The Japanese-language pages of the two Japanese-Hawaiian dailies, the *Nippu jiji* and the *Hawaii hōchi*, hailed Japan's pre-1941 victories with such headlines as "Our Units Advance Everywhere," and "Our Senda and Itakura Units Complete Occupation of P'ing Ch'ih Ch'uan." From 1937 until 1939, Hawaiian Japanese purchased 3 million yen worth of Japanese Imperial war bonds (about $882,350 at the then rate of exchange of 3.4¥ = $1) and contributed 1.2 million yen to Japan's National Defense and Soldiers' Relief Fund.[7] Although such data have never been compiled for Japanese then living on the west coast of the United States, their attitudes and financial contributions were probably quite similar.

Nor was it only the non-citizen *issei* who identified with Japan. Although *nisei* were citizens of the United States by virtue of their birth on American soil, Japan also considered them citizens because they were born of Japanese parents. Until 1924, Japan considered all Japanese abroad to be citizens unless they specifically renounced their citizenship. After 1924, Japanese born abroad had to be registered at a Japanese consulate within two weeks of their birth to retain their Japanese citizenship. Many *issei* parents found it worthwhile to give their children dual citizenship. In Hawaii, according to John Stephan,

only 8 percent (5,500 out of 66,000) of *nisei* born before 1924 had renounced their Japanese citizenship by 1933. In the same period, about 40 percent (17,800 out of 39,900) of those *nisei* born after 1924 were registered by their parents at the Japanese consulate so that they could acquire Japanese citizenship. In 1938 it was announced that children of dual citizens (*sansei*, or third generation Japanese-Americans) were eligible for registration as Japanese subjects.[8]

In addition to obtaining dual citizenship for their children, some *issei* wanted at least one of their children to be educated in Japan. Those educated in Japan were called *kibei* when they returned to Hawaii and the mainland, and those who had attended good universities in Japan (Waseda, Meiji, and Dōshisha were popular with Hawaiian Japanese) often found it easier to get white-collar jobs with Japanese banks and corporations that had branches in the United States. *Kibei*, with their greater fluency in spoken and written Japanese, would prove highly valuable to the U.S. government during World War II as language instructors, translators, and prisoner-of-war interrogators. Unfortunately, they were also the least trusted by the U.S. government.

John Stephan says there were about 40,000 foreign-born Japanese in Japan in 1938, including about 14,000 born in Hawaii.[9] As relations between Washington and Tokyo deteriorated in the spring and summer of 1941, many *kibei* returned to the United States to avoid being drafted into the Japanese army. On the other hand, some *issei* returned to Japan because they feared being enemy aliens in the United States in case war broke out. William Petersen notes that at the end of the war more than 10,000 *nisei* students, tourists, and visitors who had been trapped in Japan by the war appealed to the United States for repatriation. About half of these had lost their citizenship by serving in the Japanese army or accepting some other job that, probably unknown to them, nullified their American citizenship—for example, teaching in a public school (as opposed to a private one).[10]

One of the persons caught in this dilemma was Iva Toguri d'Aquino, a *nisei* who spent the war in Tokyo, worked for NHK (the Japanese broadcasting corporation), but refused to relinquish her American citizenship. She applied for repatriation and was returned to San Francisco in 1948 to be tried for treason as "Tokyo Rose" and was sentenced to ten years in prison.[11] On the other hand, the number of *issei* and *nisei* who returned to Japan prior to December 7, 1941, and who never attempted to live in the United States again is not known, but it probably includes several thousand.

The atmosphere in both Hawaii and the west coast of the United States immediately after Pearl Harbor was one of mass hysteria. Japanese-American fishing boats were accused of using their lights to signal to Japanese submarines and saboteurs; Japanese farmers in California were said to have planted their fields so that from the air they looked like arrows pointing to nearby airfields. Japanese fishing families living on Terminal Island in San Pedro harbor (near Long Beach, California) were the first to be forcibly evacuated between February 14 and 27, 1942. Approximately 1,500 west coast *issei* were also taken into custody by the FBI on suspicion of disloyalty; since most of those arrested were community leaders, the Japanese-American community was increasingly atomized and fearful.

Meanwhile discussions between General DeWitt, the newly appointed head of the Western Defense Command, and military and justice department figures in Washington led inexorably to the decision to move all west coast Japanese-Americans inland. The fateful Executive Order 9066, implementing this mass evacuation and incarceration, was signed by President Franklin D. Roosevelt on February 19, 1942. Between March 31 and August 7, 1942, some 110,000 Japanese-Americans (both "aliens" and "non-aliens," as the phrase of the times went) were transported to one of ten camps located in Utah, Arizona, Colorado, Wyoming, Arkansas, Idaho, and California (east of the Sierras).

Since this is a book about American attitudes, it must be reported that at the time the evacuation of Japanese-Americans was wildly popular. With the exception of a few church leaders and the pacifist Norman Thomas, even liberals such as Carey McWilliams and Earl Warren, and liberal organizations such as the ACLU, supported the mass evacuation.[12] Even when it became clear that the rumors of Japanese-American sabotage were false, people tended to use the argument put forward by Walter Lippmann in his column of February 20, 1942:

The Pacific Coast is in imminent danger of a combined attack from within and from without. . . . It is true . . . that since the outbreak of the Japanese War there has been no important sabotage on the Pacific Coast. From what we know about the fifth column in Europe, this is not, as some have liked to think, a sign that there is nothing to be feared. It is a sign that the blow is well organized, and that it is held back until it can be struck with maximum effect.[13]

There were also those in favor of evacuating the Hawaiian Islands. But since Japanese-Americans constituted 40 percent of the population and 30 percent of the labor force, this idea was soon deemed to be counterproductive to the war effort. Even on the mainland it soon proved an enormous task to house and feed 110,000 individuals when the country was mobilizing for war and factories and farms were short-handed. Thus no sooner had the Japanese been herded into camps than various schemes were set up to get them out again. Among the first to be let go were college-age students who already had been or could get themselves admitted to east coast schools. Next were able-bodied men willing and able to re-establish their families and businesses away from the west coast. For example, Iva Toguri d'Aquino's father, who had run a grocery store in Los Angeles before the war, was employed by his internment camp's administration to buy supplies. In the course of business trips across the country, he visited Chicago for the first time, and in 1943 he and his family left the camp to start another grocery store in Chicago.[14]

Still others in the camps were recruited to harvest crops, sometimes in the very areas of California from which they had been forcibly ejected. All told, before the camps were officially disbanded in December 1944, some 35,000 internees had already managed to leave in one way or another.[15] It has even been suggested by one researcher that, traumatic as it was, the camp experience hastened the Japanese-American rise into the middle-class:

The very shattering of the community's structure brought some eventual advantages. The occupational traps of the young *nisei* tending vegetable stands in Los Angeles, the seemingly unreasonable control that *issei* exerted in their families, the restrictive life in a Little Tokyo—these elements of prewar existence were reduced in importance or eliminated, together with the agricultural economy, the Japanese Associations, consular authority, and much of the informal community solidarity.[16]

Male *nisei* could also leave the camps by volunteering to serve in the U.S. Army. In early 1943, the government decided to form two all-*nisei* units to fight in Europe. (Officials were still too distrustful to send *nisei* into combat in the Pacific; but it also would have been too dangerous for the men, since they might have been mistaken for the enemy. Japanese soldiers often took the uniforms from dead American soldiers and tried to infiltrate American lines.)

The two all-*nisei* units that were formed and that distinguished themselves in combat were the 100th Infantry Battalion and the 442nd Regimental Combat Team. It is interesting, however, that when the call to arms was issued, only 1,200 *nisei* volunteered from the mainland evacuation camps, whereas more than 10,000 Hawaiian *nisei* volunteered (though ultimately only 1,500 of them were selected).[17] Perhaps no better evidence exists for the proposition that loyalty and trust comprise a two-way street.

Post–World War II Attitudes

Postwar prejudice against Japanese-Americans ebbed at about the same rate as American hatred of Japan. In the summer of 1949, when the highly publicized trial of "Tokyo Rose" took place, anti-Japanese sentiment was still strong. Even though no clear evidence was presented that treasonous statements were made over Japanese radio or that Iva Toguri d'Aquino had made them, the American public clearly believed that a "Tokyo Rose" had existed during the war and that Iva was a plausible candidate. In fact, the myth of Tokyo Rose continues to exist long after attitudes toward Iva d'Aquino have changed. She was quietly pardoned by President Ford on his last day in office, January 19, 1977, and in 1979 a well-reviewed book about Tokyo Rose appeared, which demonstrated that some of the crucial evidence at Iva's trial was perjured and coerced from Japanese then living under the occupation.[18] Nonetheless, in 1987,

Art Buchwald started a humorous column about the U.S.–Japan trade imbalance as follows:

I didn't know how serious the Japanese trade war was until I turned on the shortwave radio and heard Tokyo Rose. For those of you who missed World War II, Tokyo Rose was an outstanding enemy disc jockey who broadcast propaganda for the Japanese. Many believe that World War II would not have been as much fun without her. Rose's voice had hardly changed over the years. She said, "Hello, Mr. and Mrs. American Consumer. Your brainless leaders have started a trade war with Nippon that they cannot win. Before it's over they will rue the day they thought they could challenge the productive might of the sacred Imperial Empire." [19]

It is interesting that Buchwald calls Tokyo Rose an *enemy* disc jockey rather than an American traitor, but the link between latent hostility toward Japan and mistrust of Japanese-Americans clearly persists.

Because of this latent hostility Japanese-Americans kept a very low profile during the 1950s and 1960s on the issue of their wartime incarceration. During the latter part of World War II, the Supreme Court had twice ruled that the mass evacuation and detention of Japanese-Americans—citizen and noncitizen alike—was legal. In the cases of Minoru Yasui and Gordon Hirabayashi, the Court ruled on June 21, 1943, that the rights of Japanese-Americans were not being violated because in a wartime situation, citizens of one ethnic ancestry may be placed in a different category from other citizens in view of the danger of espionage and sabotage. [20] In the case of Fred Korematsu, the Supreme Court ruled on December 18, 1944, that his detention was legal even though he was a U.S.-born citizen because, in the words of Justice Frankfurter, "the power of the government is the power to wage war successfully."

The Supreme Court has never overruled these opinions, but on February 19, 1976, President Ford issued a proclamation rescinding Executive Order 9066. He called the original order "wrong" and declared "not only was that evacuation wrong, but Japanese Americans were and are loyal Americans." [21] In 1980,

Congress established a Commission on Wartime Relocation and Internment of Civilians that issued a report in 1983. Among other things, the report recommended that every surviving evacuee be paid $20,000 as reparations for loss of property and income.

In September 1987 a bill apologizing for the internment on behalf of the American people was passed by the House of Representatives, and a similar bill had 75 co-sponsors in the Senate. Both bills also directed federal agencies to review criminal convictions related to the internment law and provided approximately $1.2 billion to be distributed in amounts of $20,000 each to individuals who were in the camps (there are an estimated 60,000 survivors), plus at least $50 million to be set aside for an education fund to remind Americans about the forced wartime detention. It was anticipated that President Reagan would sign the bill.

Meanwhile, in early 1983 petitions were filed on behalf of Fred Korematsu, Gordon Hirabayashi, and Minoru Yasui arguing that their wartime convictions should be overturned because the government knowingly presented false evidence in their cases. On November 10, 1983, Federal District Judge Marilyn Patel ruled that Fred Korematsu's conviction should be set aside because the government had based its case on "unsubstantiated facts, distortions, and [the opinion of] one military commander whose views were seriously tainted by racism."[22] On September 24, 1987, a federal appeals court overturned Gordon Hirabayashi's conviction on similar grounds. Minoru Yasui's case was rendered moot by his death in November 1986.

A class-action suit is still pending to force the government to offer financial restitution to wartime evacuees and their descendants. If it is ever decided by the Supreme Court on its merits rather than on some technicality such as whether the statute of limitations has run out, the Supreme Court may finally overrule its wartime decisions. Such a public vindication would clearly gladden Japanese-Americans, as did the passage of the 1987 bill offering an apology. But one wonders whether financial compensation may not also provoke some hostility rather than sympathy among the public at large. When the 1987 bill was being debated in the House of Representatives, at least one Congressman commented that his father had spent the war in a Japanese prison camp and that no one had offered to compensate *his* family. Moreover, for the government to pay sizable sums of money to members of an ethnic group that is widely perceived as being prosperous and middle-class may invite the envy of ethnic groups that are less well off.

Just as American guilt over Hiroshima may have hastened the reversal of public attitudes toward Japan, so feelings of regret over the wartime incarceration of Japanese-Americans may have helped dispel the anti-Asian sentiment that was so prevalent before the war. In 1952, the Oriental Exclusion Act of 1924 was finally repealed; and although the annual immigration quota extended to all Asian nations was very low (it was revised upward only in 1965), race was finally eliminated as a barrier to naturalization. Also in 1952, the California alien land law forbidding aliens to own land was struck down.

During the 1960s and 1970s, Japanese-Americans entered the mainstream of American politics. In Hawaii, Daniel K. Inouye was elected to the U.S. House of Representatives in 1959 and to the Senate in 1962; Spark M. Matsunaga succeeded Inouye as a congressman in 1962 and moved up to the Senate in 1976. Patsy Takemoto Mink was a congresswoman from Hawaii from 1965 until 1976; Norman G. Mineta, the former mayor of San Jose, California, first became a U.S. congressman in 1974; Robert T. Matsui, a former Sacramento city councilman, was elected to congress in 1978; and Patricia Saiki became a new congresswoman from Hawaii in 1986. Samuel Ichiye Hayakawa, who first became famous as the president of San Francisco State College during the height of the Vietnam War protests, became a one-term senator from California in 1976. He won his seat by nearly a quarter of a million votes. Surely these victories are evidence of the decline of prejudice toward Japanese-Americans. At the same time, the 1960s and 1970s were also the years when American attitudes toward Japan were very favorable.

As the balance of trade with Japan has moved decisively against the United States, and as Japan seeks to recycle its surplus dollars by buying U.S. real estate and other assets, are American attitudes toward Japanese-Americans once more hardening as a reflection of attitudes toward Japan? Actually, there is very little evidence that this is the case. During the early 1970s, many people in Hawaii were fearful that Japan was buying up too much Waikiki real estate, and Japanese-Americans were accurately perceived as being more in favor of Japanese investment in the islands than other groups, causing some tensions. Between 1971 and 1975, Japan invested almost $328 million in Hawaii, including the purchase of the Sheraton-Kauai at Poipu, the Francis Brown Golf Course, the Hawaiian Regent Hotel, the Hanalei Plantation Hotel, the Sheraton-Waikiki, the Royal Hawaiian, and the Sheraton-Maui. However, by the 1980s attitudes in Hawaii had become more favorable, despite the fact that Japanese investments for 1986 alone were triple the amount spent during the 1971–75 period.

From the earliest postwar investment in 1954 to the end of 1986, Japan has invested a total of $2.6 billion in Hawaii, 94 percent of it in real estate. Japanese tourists are also important to the Hawaiian economy. In 1986, some 932,000 of them came to the islands for an average stay of six days and spent almost $300 per person per day.[23] Of course some of these tourist dollars are recycled back into Japanese-owned hotels, golf courses, and restaurants. But along the way, a fair number of Hawaiian citizens are also enriched.

Whether as a reflection of Japan's current economic power or because of their own enhanced economic status, Japanese-Americans are no longer stereotyped as gardeners, as they were before World War II.[24] Today they are more likely to be perceived as professionals such as engineers, architects, doctors, dentists, and professors. In popular literature, the Japanese Mr. Moto was succeeded, in 1977, by the Japanese-American police detective Masao Masuto. Created by Howard Fast writing under the pseudonym E. V. Cunningham, Masao Masuto works in Beverly Hills and offers the reader an attractive, up-to-date stereotype of a Japanese-American. Masuto is low-key, quiet, family-oriented, and interested in Zen meditation; however, he does not hiss, bow before his superiors, or say "Ah, so." In fact, he talks perfectly standard English. The character was probably the inspiration for a successful 1986–88 television show featuring a Japanese-American policeman called Ohara.

Ohara is portrayed by Pat Morita, a late-middle-aged Japanese-American actor who became well-known as a result of the 1984 film *The Karate Kid*. In that film he also played a Japanese-American, but a somewhat older stereotype, not speaking very good English, devoted to his bonsai trees, who works as an apartment-complex maintenance man. However, Mr. Miyagi is also a karate expert, and he takes as his pupil a young boy, freshly arrived in Los Angeles from Newark, who is being bullied by a bunch of toughs studying karate at a local *dōjō*. Miyagi teaches his charge all the traditional Japanese virtues: self-control, persistence, patience. In the course of the film we learn that Miyagi is a widower because his wife died in childbirth while in a relocation camp. Miyagi himself volunteered for one of the *nisei* units and won a Congressional Medal of Honor.

In *The Karate Kid II* we follow Miyagi and his young pupil Daniel on a trip back to Miyagi's birthplace in Okinawa, where his father is dying.* Here he becomes entangled with an old rival

---

*It is interesting that *The Karate Kid II*, like *Teahouse of the August Moon*, a popular film dating from 1956, is set in Okinawa rather than Japan itself. In *Teahouse*, made when memories of the war were still fresh, Okinawa clearly offers a way of portraying Japanese culture in a favorable light separate from the Japanese as they were during World War II. Okinawa was also victimized by the Japanese, the character played by Marlon Brando reminds us. Thus, the Okinawans can be portrayed as "good Japanese," while those on the home islands can still be perceived as "bad Japanese." One wonders if something similar is at work in *The Karate Kid II*. There is of course one glaring error in portraying Miyagi as having been born in Okinawa: this would make him an *issei*, and hence ineligible to have served in the U.S. armed forces.

who practices karate for evil ends. The young pupil meets and falls in love with a young Okinawan girl, and we are treated to a modern-day *Sayonara*—complete with lessons in the tea ceremony, *ōbon* dances, and other customs. Both *Karate Kid* films were extremely successful as movies and videotapes, leading one to suspect that—as with *Sayonara* (1954), *You Only Live Twice* (1964), and *Shōgun* (1975)—every ten years or so a new American cohort becomes fascinated with Japanese culture. It is interesting, however, that whereas in earlier novels and movies the culture contact occurred between Japanese and Americans, in *The Karate Kid* our guide to the Japanese ethos is a Japanese-American. Can it be that Japan itself is today perceived as just another modern superpower?

If relations between Japan and the United States worsen in years to come, are Japanese-Americans likely to become scapegoats once more? This strikes me as unlikely, if only for the reason that the injustice of their World War II treatment serves as a constant reminder that it must not happen again. But another reason why I do not believe that Japanese-Americans will in the future be treated as an undifferentiated racial group is their rate of intermarriage with non-Japanese. While no complete figures are available, surveys indicate that more than half of all *sansei* (third generation) are marrying non-Japanese spouses—a figure considerably higher than the current rate of Jewish outmarriage, which hovers at 33 percent.[25]

This is not to suggest that Japanese-Americans will disappear, but for many their Japaneseness will become merely one component of a mixed ethnic identity. Just as some Americans now say they are part Scottish, part Chippewa, and part Italian, others will be saying they are part Japanese, part Chinese, and part Swedish. I have always wondered at the tendency of Japanese-Americans to keep track of their generations away from the homeland—*issei, nisei, sansei,* and so forth—but perhaps this was not surprising, considering the different burdens placed on each of these generations (one could not become U.S. citizens, the others could be dual citizens). I suspect, however, that this generational countdown will not extend much beyond the fourth and fifth generations, as Japanese-Americans join the ethnic stew that has already given the world the *mushirito* (a cross between Chinese *mushiro* and the burrito) and a kind of Lebanese taco called the *fajita pita.*

TEN

Conclusion

WHAT, IN THE final analysis, do all of these various impressions and arguments add up to? In the last forty-five years Americans have thought of the Japanese as warlike and cruel, as charming and artistic, as business-oriented and clever. We have been hostile toward the Japanese; remorseful over Hiroshima; condescending, admiring, wary, irritated, and baffled in the face of Japanese culture. To some extent all these attitudes coexist in the United States, since different groups of Americans are drawing upon different experiences with Japan to form their stereotypes. Many of the stereotypes have their roots in specific events so that one cannot call them entirely erroneous, although like all stereotypes they tend to be one-dimensional. One purpose of this study is to promote a more stereoscopic vision of Japan by summarizing and analyzing some of the events that have molded American opinions during the last forty-five years.

The Limitations of National Character

Another purpose of this study is to argue that national stereotypes are based on specific impressions of people and events rather than on something immutable known as national character. If the latter were the deciding factor, we would be at a loss to explain the frequent and rapid changes that American perceptions of the Japanese have undergone. In the first chapter, I described how the concept of national character was, in fact, developed during World War II as a curious amalgam of Freudian insights, anthropological methods developed in the study of small, primitive tribes, and the necessity of conducting psychological warfare against our enemies. The language of national character studies was never very exact, and its hypotheses have frequently been dismissed as tautological. Since World War II one social scientist, Anthony Wallace, has demonstrated that in two different societies only between 28 and 37 percent of the adult populations possessed the "modal personalities" of those cultures (where modal personality was defined in terms of 21 parameters, which still left a great deal of room for diversity in other personality traits).[1] Another social scientist, Alex Inkeles, has presented some very persuasive statistics demonstrating that the perceptions and values of certain social groups—for example, bureaucrats and factory workers—resemble one another cross-culturally more than they resemble those of other groups in their own society. In other words, a factory worker in the United States may have more in common with a factory worker in Japan than with an American banker, professor, or farmhand.[2] If this is so, then the concept of national character has been dealt a formidable blow.

I have also tried to argue in this book that Americans may have fixed in their heads a sort of generalized "Asian" stereotype. This stereotype would include certain physical features—slanted, almond-shaped eyes, black straight hair, olive complexion, short stature—and certain personality and cultural traits—Asians are soft-spoken, sometimes evasive, polite, quiet, reserved, family-oriented, hard-working. This generalized stereotype has been attached to *all* the Asian groups with whom Americans have come into contact: Chinese, Japanese, Koreans,

Vietnamese, Thai, Laotians. If it has any basis at all, it is probably only that Americans feel themselves to be bigger, brasher, louder, and more extroverted than Asians. The generalized Asian stereotype also comes in positive and negative versions, depending on how the United States feels about a particular nation at a given time. When Americans were at war with Japan, quietness turned into deviousness, and stoicism (another trait commonly ascribed to all Asians) became cruelty. When Americans were fighting the Chinese in Korea, the same negative attributes were attached to them, whereas the Japanese suddenly became our trustworthy, hard-working, gentle allies.

Not only does the Asian stereotype have both positive and negative valences, but there is some evidence that when it is applied to the two major countries in East Asia, China and Japan, the positive and negative are kept in balance. That is to say, when China is up, Japan will be down, and vice versa. In recent history, Americans have rarely held either simultaneously positive or simultaneously negative views of both countries. Instead, during World War II, China rode high and Japan was low in our estimation. After 1949, with the Communists' victory in China and the Korean War, the judgments were reversed. In the mid-1960s, after a brief downturn in American views of the Japanese following the Security Treaty riots, opinions of Japan were highly favorable, while opinions of China, then embroiled in the Cultural Revolution, were generally negative. I omit here the views of the political left in the United States and Europe, which became infatuated with China *because of* the Cultural Revolution. This segment of public opinion only turned against China in 1972, when the so-called pragmatists appeared to regain control in Peking and invited Richard Nixon to visit—events that the general public hailed and that led it once again to view China in a favorable light.

With the death of Mao in 1976 and the upheavals around the Gang of Four, American attitudes toward China tended once again to revert to the Fu Manchu stereotype; meanwhile Japan rode high in our estimation. Yet by the mid-1980s, with a liberalizing regime in China and a worsening trade deficit with Japan, the U.S. stereotype of China became favorable once more and the images of Japan became almost as harsh and threatening as they were during World War II.

The Situational Approach

The rapidity with which the images of Japan and China have changed since World War II has led me to set aside the whole notion of national character as a guide to understanding popular attitudes. If there is such a thing as national character, it cannot be subject to such frequent reversals. It strikes me as more accurate, as well as more hopeful, to assume that national stereotypes are based on immediate impressions of people and events rather than upon some deepseated, immutable force known as national character. One hopeful conclusion that might be drawn from the view that national stereotypes have their roots in specific events is that Japan and other nations have only to behave well on the international scene in order to be loved and admired by everyone. In other words, handsome is as handsome does. Unfortunately, the matter is not so simple. Cultural contact is a two-way street, and a nation's behavior is inevitably conditioned by the interpretation it places on the actions of other nations. What the United States does, no matter how we ourselves choose to interpret it, is bound to be interpreted differently by others and to have an impact on the behavior of other nations like Japan. In terms of the history of the two nations, for example, Noam Chomsky was at least partly correct when he argued that U.S. efforts to embargo Japan during the 1930s helped produce anti-American and expansionist sentiments among the Japanese, which in turn helped inflame Americans still further. Whether this spiral of mutual distrust could have been halted by men of good will, and who should bear the blame for the war that actually followed, are not my concern here—though it is worth pointing out that arguments wholly in favor of one side or the other are always likely to be biased, and often are skewing history in order to make a current political point. (Chomsky argues that Japan was not fascist and expansionist in the 1930s, but that the United States was, and is.) But spirals of mutual interaction and perception exist today, just as they did in the past, and the way these may develop in the future should be of concern to all Americans and Japanese.

A case in point can be drawn from the realm of trade. Throughout the decade 1975–85, the United States had a growing trade deficit with Japan. While all the economic ramifications of this were not well understood by the average American, it is significant that the *New York Times* / CBS News poll of July 1985 found that 87 percent of the Americans interviewed knew that Japan sold more to the United States than it bought from it. By contrast, a parallel poll conducted in Japan found that 36 percent of the Japanese questioned thought the reverse was true, that Japan bought more from the United States than it sold.[3] More important than general awareness of the trade issue, however, was the fact that various industries in the United States were feeling the effects of foreign competition. Nor was this competition always from Japan. The cries of outrage by the U.S. textile industry, which used to be directed against Japan in the 1950s and 1960s, were in the 1980s being directed at imports from China, Hong Kong, and Korea. Pressure to restrict Japanese imports in the 1980s came primarily from the semiconductor, steel, and automobile industries. In automobiles, for example, Japanese cars had moved from 6.7 percent of the U.S. market in 1974 to around 20 percent throughout the 1980s; and this last figure was artificially low because of a "voluntary" export quota maintained by the Japanese.

Members of the Reagan administration warned repeatedly that U.S. imposition of tariffs against foreign goods would only provoke retaliation by other nations, and that a rollback in various imports such as clothing and automobiles would raise the prices American consumers pay for those products. They also pointed out that any sort of trade war would severely damage

U.S. agriculture, which in 1983 shipped 27 percent of its exported feed grains and corn, 26 percent of its exported cotton, and 20 percent of its exported soybeans to Japan. Overall, Japan was the United States's leading customer for agricultural exports, buying in 1983 some $6,251 million worth of goods.[4] Nonetheless, it remains entirely possible that sometime during the late 1980s a trade war with Japan will develop, with each country's citizens coming to see the other as the root cause of all its problems—a situation dangerously reminiscent of the 1930s.

A different example of current interaction and potential misunderstanding lies in the realm of mutual security. Under the terms of the mutual security treaty between Japan and the United States, the United States promises to defend Japan in case of attack by a third power; and since the United States is one of those nations possessing nuclear weapons, it effectively shields Japan from nuclear blackmail or from the need to build its own nuclear deterrent. Partly as a result of the trade imbalance, the United States began in the late 1970s to press Japan to do more toward its own defense. Japan, in turn, cited the famous "anti-war" clause of its constitution (Article 9, forced on Japan by the American occupiers), in which it renounced forever "land, sea, and air forces, as well as other war potential."

Unfortunately, the Japanese were caught in a dilemma. If they were to heed U.S. demands that they increase their defense expenditures, China, Southeast Asian countries, and perhaps even the United States itself might become uneasy at the sight of a remilitarized Japan. On the other hand, if they persisted in spending less than 1 percent of their annual GNP on defense while the United States spent approximately 7 percent of its budget on military needs, American cries that Japan was not carrying its fair share of the burden would probably increase.[5] In mid-1985, public opinion polls found that 82 percent of the Japanese and 70 percent of the Americans interviewed were opposed to Japan's acquiring nuclear weapons. But despite the existence of the security treaty, 54 percent of the Japanese surveyed did not think the

United States would actually come to their defense if Japan were attacked.[6] Such ambivalent and contradictory feelings on the part of both nations make it likely that mutual security will continue to be a delicate and volatile issue. If Americans were to become tired of paying for the defense of what is now a rich and powerful nation, they might be tempted to say to Japan, "Look to your own interests." Such a development, however, would almost surely lead to full-scale Japanese rearmament; and this, in turn, would have an enormous impact on Americans' (and other nations') perceptions of Japan.

Still another source of potential danger is Japan's tendency to think of itself as a nation somehow set apart from the rest of mankind. During World War II this notion was bolstered by a state ideology which claimed that the Japanese emperor was descended directly from the Sun Goddess, and that the Japanese people had a manifest destiny to conquer and rule other Asian nations. In the 1980s, Japan's renewed economic strength produced another form of this ideology: namely, that the Japanese owe their success to their racial purity. Prime Minister Nakasone deeply shocked Americans when, on September 22, 1986, he was quoted as saying to a group of his supporters that Japan's recent achievements were the result of its homogenous society, whereas the mental level in the United States was lower because "there are blacks, Puerto Ricans and Hispanics."[7]

Nakasone subsequently apologized and claimed to have been misquoted and misunderstood. But there was considerable feeling in the United States among those knowledgeable about Japan that Nakasone's remarks were no accident. James Fallows, in an article published shortly before Nakasone's fateful "slip-of-the-tongue," noted:

Their forty-year recovery represents a triumph of a system and a people, but I think many Japanese see it as the victory of a *pure* people, which by definition no inferior or mixed-blood race can match. . . . But to me, its ethic of exclusion is the least loveable thing about this society. And I hope, as the Japanese reflect upon their victories, that they congratulate themselves for diligence, sacrifice, and teamwork, not for remaining "pure."[8]

Mr. Fallows might have added a warning that for the Japanese to persist in an ideology of racial purity setting them apart from the rest of the world is also to invite that world to turn *its* back on Japan. Thus Japanese exclusivity could produce a form of international lock-out that would reinforce those feelings of specialness, and this in turn could set off a further fateful spiral of ill will and misunderstanding.

Cultivating Multiple Images

Given the complex relationship between international behavior and the stereotypes of nations, there can be no easy answer to how a particular nation—say, Japan—can maintain a favorable image in the eyes of another nation, such as the United States. Certainly one partial solution is "handsome is as handsome does." Good relations between two countries at the governmental and business levels generally contribute to favorable popular images, while states of war, trade embargoes, or other international tensions promote unflattering popular images. But if such real events shape popular stereotypes, it is also true that, once stereotypes take hold, they can shape international events. It is important, therefore, to ensure that a single unfortunate turn in the international arena (Japanese reluctance to lower tariff barriers against American rice and oranges, say, or American restrictions on the import of Japanese cars) does not begin a spiral of ill will. One way of helping prevent such a spiral is to promote and publicize a multiplicity of stereotypes. In this respect the United States and Japan are very fortunate in having known many favorable images of one another in the course of their relations. For Americans, these include their memories of the occupation, their infatuation with things Japanese during the late 1950s and early 1960s, and their current admiration for Japanese industrial products. Japan is not nearly so fortunate when it comes to its image in China and Southeast Asia. There, bitter memories of the war linger and are only gradually being offset by admiration for Japan's postwar industrial growth, which is often envied and feared.

A multiplicity of images makes it more difficult for a particular stereotype to dominate one nation's perspective on another nation. "The Japanese are sneaky and cruel" may be one residue of World War II. "Yes, but the Japanese are also kind and gentle," is likely to be the response of someone who was there during the occupation. "The Japanese are artistic and non-materialistic" may be the impression of a 1960s visitor. "The Japanese are hard-driving businessmen," says the tourist of the 1980s. No doubt each of these images contains, or contained, a kernel of truth; but their multiplicity and impermanence should make us cautious about accepting any one of them as either fixed or wholly accurate. Americans should also be wary of the assertions some Japanese (including Japanese scholars) make about their own culture, since these are often matters of domestic debate—or what the Japanese think Americans want to hear. In the final analysis, Americans would do well to cultivate a permanent suspicion of any sentence that begins "The Japanese are . . . ," with the possible exception of the following. The Japanese are an interesting and talented people, fully as diverse and capable of change as we credit ourselves with being.

Notes

Notes

PREFACE

1. "To China, With Love," *Commentary*, vol. 55, no. 6 (June 1973), 37–45.
2. *American Attitudes Toward Japan, 1941–1975.*

CHAPTER 1

1. Foster Rhea Dulles, *Yankees and Samurai* (New York: Harper, 1965), pp. 68–69.
2. Elizabeth Stevenson, *Lafcadio Hearn* (New York: Macmillan, 1961), p. 256.
3. Lafcadio Hearn, *Japan: An Attempt at Interpretation* (New York: Macmillan, 1924 [copyright 1904]), pp. 502, 503.
4. Stevenson, *Lafcadio Hearn*, p. 268.
5. Nathan Glazer, "From Ruth Benedict to Herman Kahn: The Postwar Japanese Image in the American Mind," in Akira Iriye, ed., *Mutual Images: Essays in American-Japanese Relations* (Cambridge, Mass.: Harvard University Press, 1975); Ruth Benedict, *The Chrysanthemum and the Sword* (Boston: Houghton Mifflin, 1946), pp. 2–3.
6. John Embree, *Suye Mura: A Japanese Village* (Chicago: University of Chicago Press, 1939).
7. Geoffrey Gorer, "Themes in Japanese Culture," New York Academy of Sciences *Transactions*, series 2, vol. 5, no. 5 (Mar. 1943), 119, 118.
8. John Embree, "Standard Error and Japanese Character: A Note on Political Interpretation," *World Politics*, vol. 2, no. 3 (Apr. 1950), 442.

9. Douglas Haring, "Japanese National Character: Cultural Anthropology, Psychoanalysis, and History," *Yale Review*, Spring 1953, p. 386.

10. Embree, "Standard Error," p. 443. See also Richard H. Minear, "The Wartime Studies of Japanese National Character," *The Japan Interpreter*, vol. 13, no. 1 (Summer 1980), 36–59; John Dower, *War Without Mercy: Race and Power in the Pacific War* (New York: Pantheon, 1986), pp. 118–39, 336–41.

11. Jacobus tenBroek, Edward N. Barnhart, and Floyd W. Matson, *Prejudice, War and the Constitution* (Berkeley: University of California Press, 1954), p. 23.

12. Weston LaBarre, "Some Observations on Character Structure in the Orient: The Japanese and the Chinese (Parts I and II)," *Psychiatry*, vol. 8, no. 3 (1945), 319–42; vol. 9, no. 3 (1946), 215–38; vol. 9, no. 4 (1946), 375–95.

13. Elizabeth Gray Vining, *Windows for the Crown Prince* (New York: Lippincott, 1952), p. 315.

14. *New York Times Book Review*, Nov. 10, 1946, p. 56.

15. For the results of the poll, see *New York Times*, Aug. 6, 1985, pp. 1, A8; Aug. 13, 1985, pp. 1, D6.

16. *Ibid.*, Aug. 13, 1985, p. D6.

17. Glazer, "From Ruth Benedict to Herman Kahn."

18. Ian Fleming, *You Only Live Twice* (New York: New American Library, 1965), p. 35.

CHAPTER 2

1. Gregory D. Black and Clayton R. Koppes, "OWI Goes to the Movies," *Foreign Service Journal*, Aug. 1974, pp. 18–23, 29–30. Also in *Prologue: The Journal of the National Archives*, 6 (1974), 44–59.

2. Norman Mailer, *The Naked and the Dead* (New York: New American Library, c. 1948), p. 37.

3. *Ibid.*, pp. 385, 544.

4. John Hersey, *Into the Valley* (New York: Knopf, 1944), pp. 55, 20–21.

5. Mailer, *The Naked and the Dead*, p. 554.

6. *Ibid.*, p. 196.

7. Richard Tregaskis, *Guadalcanal Diary* (New York: Random House, 1943), pp. 80, 81, 83.

8. *Time*, Sept. 28, 1942, p. 37.

9. Tregaskis, *Guadalcanal Diary*, p. 239.

10. John Hersey, *Men on Bataan* (New York: Knopf, 1942), p. 146.

11. Tregaskis, *Guadalcanal Diary*, pp. 54–55.

12. For an interesting account of the whole Prange book operation, see Roger Pineau, "A New Skirmish over Pacific War Saga," *Christian Science Monitor*, Dec. 7, 1982.
13. Gordon W. Prange, *At Dawn We Slept* (New York: McGraw-Hill, 1981), p. ix.
14. *Ibid.*, p. 202.
15. *Ibid.*, p. xi. This material was subsequently published as *Pearl Harbor: The Verdict of History* (New York: McGraw-Hill, 1986).
16. John Toland, *Infamy: Pearl Harbor and Its Aftermath* (New York: Doubleday, 1982), p. xv.
17. *Ibid.*
18. *Ibid.*, p. 324.
19. "Pappy" [Colonel Gregory] Boyington, *Baa Baa Black Sheep* (New York: Putnam, 1958), p. 276.
20. *Ibid.*, pp. 90, 92, 105.
21. *Ibid.*, p. 269.
22. *Ibid.*, p. 307.
23. *Ibid.*, p. 333.
24. William Manchester, *Goodbye Darkness: A Memoir of the Pacific War* (New York: Dell, 1982), p. 192.
25. *Ibid.*, p. 268.
26. *Ibid.*, p. 392.
27. *Ibid.*, p. 223.
28. *Ibid.*, pp. 245, 320, 387.
29. Studs Terkel, *"The Good War": An Oral History of World War II* (New York: Pantheon, 1984), p. 561.
30. *Ibid.*, pp. 60, 61.
31. *Ibid.*, p. 82.
32. *Ibid.*, p. 96.
33. Theodore H. White, "The Danger from Japan," *New York Times Magazine*, July 28, 1985, p. 20.
34. *Ibid.*, pp. 57, 38.
35. *American Attitudes Toward Japan* (Washington, D.C.: American Enterprise Institute, 1975), p. 31.

CHAPTER 3

1. *New York Times*, Aug. 7, 1945, p. 1.
2. *New York Times Magazine*, Aug. 1, 1965, p. 9.
3. Paul W. Tibbets, Jr., as told to Wesley Price, "How to Drop an A-Bomb," *Saturday Evening Post*, June 8, 1946, p. 18.
4. *New York Times*, Aug. 10, 1945, p. 1.

5. Forty years later the official Japanese figure of confirmed deaths—including those who died in subsequent years of A-bomb-related causes—was 116,271 (*Japan Times Weekly*, July 20, 1985).

6. See Hersey, *Into the Valley*, p. 56.

7. See Robert Jay Lifton, *Death in Life* (New York: Random House, 1967). I say "appears" because Lifton does not identify most of the people he interviewed by name and one must therefore deduce his overlap with authors Hersey, Jungk, and Hachiya from internal evidence—namely, the life-histories themselves.

8. *New York Times Magazine*, July 31, 1955, p. 21.

9. In 1985, a book updating the lives of the Hiroshima Maidens was published but did not become a best-seller: Rodney Barker, *The Hiroshima Maidens* (New York: Viking).

10. William Bradford Huie, *The Hiroshima Pilot* (New York: Pocket Books, 1965), p. 343.

11. *New York Times*, Mar. 13, 1969, p. 44.

12. Terkel, "*The Good War*," p. 183.

CHAPTER 4

1. U.S. Department of State, "Basic Initial Post-Surrender Directive," in Jon Livingston, Joe Moore, and Felicia Oldfather, eds., *The Japan Reader*, vol. 2 (New York: Pantheon, 1973), p. 7.

2. Joseph C. Grew, *Ten Years in Japan* (New York: Simon and Schuster, 1944), p. xi.

3. Otto Tolischus, "God-Emperor: Key to a Nation," *New York Times Magazine*, Aug. 19, 1945, pp. 8, 33.

4. T. A. Bisson, "The Japanese Discuss Their 'Sacred Mission,'" [review of Otto Tolischus, *Through Japanese Eyes*] *New York Times Book Review*, Apr. 15, 1945, p. 6; "Japan's Strategy of Revival," *New Republic*, Aug. 27, 1945, pp. 242–43.

5. Quoted in Andrew Roth, *Dilemma in Japan* (Boston: Little, Brown, 1945), p. 36.

6. *Ibid.*, p. 35.

7. *New York Times*, Aug. 11, 1945, p. 4.

8. Courtney Whitney, *MacArthur: His Rendezvous with History* (New York: Knopf, 1956), p. 284. Interestingly enough, MacArthur's own description is almost word-for-word the same. See Douglas MacArthur, *Reminiscences* (New York: McGraw-Hill, 1964), p. 288.

9. Vining, *Windows for the Crown Prince*, pp. 157, 208.

10. Mark Gayn, *Japan Diary* (New York: Sloane, 1948), pp. 501, 6, 504.

11. R. C. Kramer, "Japan Must Compete," *Fortune*, June 1947, p. 112.

12. Quoted *ibid.*, p. 112.

13. Sidney Shalett, "Why We're Trading with the Enemy," *Saturday Evening Post*, July 12, 1947, p. 25.

14. Helen Mears, "We're Giving Japan 'Democracy,' but She Can't Earn Her Living," *Saturday Evening Post*, June 18, 1949, p. 10.

15. "Two-billion Dollar Failure in Japan: Economic Report on SCAP," *Fortune*, Apr. 1949, pp. 67–73, 204–8.

16. *Ibid.*, p. 204. For MacArthur's reply, see *Fortune*, June 1949, pp. 74–75, 188–204.

17. Vining, *Windows*, p. 169.

18. Robert B. Textor, *Failure in Japan* (New York: John Day, 1951), pp. 47, 48, 93.

19. *Ibid.*, p. 166.

20. U.S. Congress, Senate, *Hearings before the Committee on Armed Services and the Committee on Foreign Relations to Conduct an Inquiry into the Military Situation in the Far East and the Facts Surrounding the Relief of General of the Army Douglas MacArthur from his Assignments in that Area*, part 1, 82nd Congress, 1st session (Washington, D.C.: U.S. Government Printing Office, 1951), p. 312.

21. John Gunther, *The Riddle of MacArthur* (New York: Harper, 1951), p. xiv.

22. *Ibid.*, pp. 51, 115.

23. *Ibid.*, pp. 229–31.

24. Edward Friedman and Mark Selden, *America's Asia: Dissenting Essays on Asian-American Relations* (New York: Vintage, 1971), p. xi.

25. Noam Chomsky, *American Power and the New Mandarins* (New York: Pantheon, 1969), pp. 191–92.

26. Richard H. Minear, *Victors' Justice: The Tokyo War Crimes Trial* (Tokyo: Charles Tuttle Co., 1972), p. xii. (Published by Princeton University Press in the United States.)

27. *Ibid.*, p. x.

28. Interview with James Reston, *New York Times*, Oct. 13, 1974, p. 35.

CHAPTER 5

1. Boyington, *Baa Baa Black Sheep*, p. 309.

2. Gayn, *Japan Diary*, p. 234.

3. Statistics for 1965–85 from *Jinkō dōtai tōkei* (Vital Statistics of Japan), were compiled for me by William Wetherall.

4. Stevenson, *Lafcadio Hearn*, p. 228.

5. Hearn, *Japan*, p. 394.
6. James A. Michener, *Sayonara* (Greenwich, Conn.: Fawcett, 1964 [copyright 1953, 1954]), pp. 97, 106.
7. *Ibid.*, pp. 127–28.
8. *Ibid.*, pp. 120–21.
9. *Ibid.*, pp. 7, 11.
10. Gwen Terasaki, *Bridge to the Sun* (Chapel Hill: University of North Carolina Press, 1957), pp. 7, 20, 40, 252.
11. Alice Ekert-Rotholz, *The Time of the Dragons* (New York: Viking, 1958), p. 29.
12. *Ibid.*, p. 295. Readers of Japanese will recognize that something odd is being done to the language here. *Ki-no-doku*, as it should be romanized, would never be used by anyone in this context, and the translation is ludicrous.
13. *Ibid.*, p. 436.
14. As quoted in Ronald Bell, ed., *The Japan Experience* (New York: Weatherhill, 1973), p. 217.
15. Oliver Statler, *Japanese Inn* (New York: Random House, 1961), p. 159.
16. Kate Millett, "A Personal Discovery," *Ms.* magazine, Mar. 1973, p. 57.

CHAPTER 6

1. Statler, *Japanese Inn*, pp. 323, 46.
2. Gunther, *The Riddle of MacArthur*, p. 86.
3. James A. Michener, "Japan," *Holiday*, Aug. 1952, p. 32.
4. *New York Times*, Dec. 27, 1951, p. 18.
5. *Ibid.*, Sept. 8, 1954, p. 40.
6. *Ibid.*, Dec. 14, 1954, p. 45.
7. *Ibid.*
8. Faubion Bowers, "Concerning Kabuki," *Saturday Review of Literature*, Feb. 27, 1954, p. 25.
9. *New York Times*, Feb. 28, 1954, sec. 2, p. 4.
10. *New York Times Magazine*, July 11 and 18, 1954.
11. Elizabeth Gray Vining, *Return to Japan* (New York: Lippincott, 1960), p. 165.
12. John Marquand, *Stopover Tokyo* (Boston: Little, Brown, 1957), pp. 22, 228, 219–20.
13. Statler, *Japanese Inn*, p. 363.
14. Fleming, *You Only Live Twice*, p. 99. The notion that Japan has an

exceptionally high suicide rate is another mistaken stereotype. In 1964, for example, Japan ranked tenth in terms of frequency of suicide, after West Berlin, Hungary, Austria, Denmark, Czechoslovakia, West Germany, Finland, Sweden, and Switzerland. See George De Vos, *Socialization for Achievement* (Berkeley: University of California Press, 1973), p. 455.

15. Fleming, *You Only Live Twice*, p. 79.
16. *Ibid.*, p. 11.

CHAPTER 7

1. *New York Times Book Review*, June 22, 1975, p. 5.
2. Henry Smith, ed., *Learning from Shōgun: Japanese History and Western Fantasy* (Santa Barbara: University of California, Santa Barbara, Program in Asian Studies, 1980), p. 15. See also *Christian Science Monitor*, Sept. 15, 1980, p. 23.
3. Henry Smith, *Learning from Shōgun*, p. 15.
4. *Ibid.*
5. James Clavell, *Shōgun* (New York: Dell, 1976), p. 140.
6. *Ibid.*, p. 508.   7. *Ibid.*, p. 544.
8. *Ibid.*, p. 413.   9. *Ibid.*, pp. 496, 498.
10. *Ibid.*, pp. 365, 370, 602, 705.
11. *Ibid.*, p. 883.
12. However, sales figures for 1985 indicate that 1,160,000 paperback copies of *The Miko* were sold. *Publishers Weekly*, Mar. 14, 1986, p. 33.
13. Eric Van Lustbader, *The Ninja* (New York: Fawcett Crest, 1981), pp. 306–7.
14. *New York Times Book Review*, May 18, 1980, p. 44.
15. Lustbader, *The Ninja*, pp. 156, 159, 160.
16. For the mini-history of MITI, see Eric Van Lustbader, *The Miko* (New York: Villard, 1984), pp. 160–80. This material could only have come from Chalmers Johnson, *MITI and the Japanese Miracle* (Stanford, Calif.: Stanford University Press, 1982).
17. Lustbader, *The Miko*, pp. 32–33.
18. *Ibid.*, p. 65.   19. *Ibid.*, p. 309.
20. *Ibid.*, p. 391.   21. *Ibid.*, p. 438.
22. Lustbader, *The Ninja*, p. 140.
23. *Ibid.*, pp. 146–47.
24. Della Femina later used the tag-line as the title of his memoirs. See Jerry Della Femina, *From Those Wonderful Folks Who Gave You Pearl Harbor* (New York: Simon & Schuster, 1970).
25. Lee Iacocca, *An Autobiography* (New York: Bantam, 1984), p. 315.

CHAPTER 8

1. John Davenport, "In Japan It's 'Jimmu Keiki,'" *Fortune*, July 1957, p. 107.
2. *Business Week*, Dec. 17, 1949, p. 106.
3. *Ibid.*, Apr. 8, 1950, p. 66.   4. *Ibid.*, July 7, 1951, p. 148.
5. *Ibid.*, Sept. 7, 1957, p. 158.   6. *Ibid.*, Sept. 24, 1955, p. 150.
7. *Newsweek*, Dec. 2, 1974, p. 26.
8. These figures come from the complete *Los Angeles Times* poll, no. 99. Stories dealing with the poll appeared in the *Los Angeles Times*, Oct. 24 and 25, 1985.
9. *Business Week*, June 6, 1953, p. 144.
10. *Ibid.*, Apr. 25, 1953, p. 161.
11. D. L. Cohn, "Southern Cotton and Japan," *Atlantic Monthly*, Aug. 1956, p. 55; and *Business Week*, Sept. 24, 1955.
12. *Business Week*, Nov. 12, 1966, p. 140.
13. See I. M. Destler, Haruhiro Fukui, and Hideo Sato, *The Textile Wrangle: Conflict in Japanese-American Relations, 1969–71* (Ithaca, N.Y.: Cornell University Press, 1979).
14. Interestingly enough, Vogel's book was quickly translated into Japanese and became a huge best-seller there. The Japanese have long been interested in what foreigners think of them, although in this regard they are not so different from other nations: Luigi Barzini's and Alistair Cooke's books about the United States held a similar appeal for Americans. But no doubt an added attraction of Vogel's book to the Japanese was the fact that a foreigner—and an American at that—was holding them up as a model of excellence.
15. William G. Ouchi, *Theory Z* (New York: Avon, 1982), p. 29.
16. *Ibid.*, p. 167.
17. *Ibid.*, p. 164.
18. David Halberstam, *The Reckoning* (New York: Morrow, 1986), pp. 727–28.

CHAPTER 9

1. Quoted in tenBroek, Barnhart, and Matson, *Prejudice, War and the Constitution*, p. 351, n. 65.
2. *Ibid.*, p. 15.
3. In 1881, King Kalakaua visited Japan and suggested that his niece marry a Japanese prince in order to create a bond between Japanese and Hawaiian royalty. The Emperor Meiji politely declined the offer. John J.

Stephan, *Hawaii Under the Rising Sun* (Honolulu: University of Hawaii Press, 1984), pp. 17–18.

4. Robert A. Wilson and Bill Hosokawa, *East to America* (New York: Morrow, 1980), pp. 140–41.

5. *Ibid.*, p. 143.

6. William Petersen, *Japanese Americans* (New York: Random House, 1971), p. 20.

7. Stephan, *Hawaii*, pp. 28, 33.

8. *Ibid.*, p. 24. It was this situation that lay behind General DeWitt's statement "A Jap's a Jap." As Senator Tom Stewart argued, "A Jap born on our soil is a subject of Japan under Japanese law; therefore, he owes allegiance to Japan." Quoted in tenBroek *et al.*, *Prejudice*, p. 87.

9. Stephan, *Hawaii*, p. 41.

10. Petersen, *Japanese Americans*, p. 99, n. 31.

11. Masayo Duus, *Tokyo Rose: Orphan of the Pacific* (Tokyo: Kodansha, 1979).

12. Petersen, *Japanese Americans*, pp. 75–79.

13. Quoted in Dennis M. Ogawa, *From Japs to Japanese: An Evolution of Japanese-American Stereotypes* (Berkeley, Calif.: McCutchan, 1971), p. 20.

14. Duus, *Tokyo Rose*, p. 20.

15. Wilson and Hosokawa, *East to America*, p. 219.

16. Petersen, *Japanese Americans*, p. 126.

17. Wilson and Hosokawa, *East to America*, p. 228.

18. Duus, *Tokyo Rose*.

19. Art Buchwald, "U.S. vs. the Land of the Rising Sony," *Los Angeles Times*, Apr. 7, 1987.

20. Wilson and Hosokawa, *East to America*, p. 252.

21. *Ibid.*, p. 297.

22. *San Francisco Examiner*, Nov. 11, 1983.

23. For the investment figures, see *A Listing of Foreign Investment in Hawaii*, International Business Series No. 47 (Honolulu: State of Hawaii, Department of Planning and Economic Development, Dec. 31, 1986); and for the tourism figures see *Study of Japanese Winter Visitors to Hawaii, 1987* (Honolulu: Hawaii Visitors Bureau, Feb. 1987).

24. Ogawa, *From Japs to Japanese*, p. 35.

25. Wilson and Hosokawa, *East to America*, p. 299.

CHAPTER 10

1. Anthony Wallace, "The Modal Personality Structure of the Tuscarora Indians as Revealed by the Rorschach Test," *Bulletin*, Bureau of American

Ethnology, no. 150; and "Individual Differences and Cultural Uniformities," *American Sociological Review*, 17 (1952), 747–50.

2. Alex Inkeles, "Industrial Man: The Relation of Status to Experience, Perception, and Value," *American Journal of Sociology*, 66 (July 1960), 1–31; and *Becoming Modern: Individual Change in Six Developing Countries* (Cambridge, Mass.: Harvard University Press, 1974). Notwithstanding William Ouchi's and others' depiction of Japanese workers as happily embedded in family-like companies, there is plenty of evidence to support Inkeles's arguments. For a portrait of Japanese autoworkers that strongly resembles studies of American autoworkers, see Satoshi Kamata, *Japan in the Passing Lane* (New York: Pantheon, 1982). Cf. Ely Chinoy, *Automobile Workers and the American Dream* (Boston: Beacon, 1955).

3. *New York Times*, Aug. 13, 1985, p. D6.

4. Japan Institute for Social and Economic Affairs, *Japan 1984: An International Comparison* (Tokyo: Keizai Kōhō Center, 1984), p. 18.

5. Chalmers Johnson, "Reflections on the Dilemma of Japanese Defense," *Asian Survey*, vol. 26, no. 5 (May 1986), 101–16.

6. *New York Times*, Aug. 6, 1985, p. A8.

7. See *Japan Times Weekly*, Oct. 11, 1986, p. 1.

8. James Fallows, "The Japanese Are Different from You and Me," *Atlantic Monthly* (Sept. 1986), p. 41.

Index

Library of Congress Cataloging-in-Publication Data

Johnson, Sheila K.
The Japanese through American eyes / Sheila K. Johnson.
p.   cm.
Includes index.
ISBN 0-8047-1449-5 (alk. paper)
1. Japan—Foreign public opinion, American.   2. Public opinion—
United States.   I. Title.
DS806.J64   1988
952.04—dc 19   88-2375
                                                    CIP